Skyhorse Publishing books may be purchased in bulk at special discounts for sales promotion, corporate gifts, fund-raising, or educational purposes. Special editions can also be created to specifications. For details, contact the Special Sales Department, Skyhorse Publishing, 307 West 36th Street, 11th Floor, New York, NY 10018 or info@skyhorsepublishing.com.

Skyhorse® and Skyhorse Publishing® are registered trademarks of Skyhorse Publishing, Inc., a Delaware corporation.

Visit our website at www.skyhorsepublishing.com.

10 9 8 7 6

Library of Congress Cataloging-in-Publication Data is available on file.

Design by Melissa Gerber
Images used under license by Shutterstock.com

Print ISBN: 978-1-5107-7473-5
eBook ISBN: 978-1-5107-7511-4

Printed in the United States of America

Nobody Wants Your Sh*t

the
art of
decluttering
before
you die

Messie Condo

Skyhorse Publishing, Inc

Contents

CHAPTER 5:
LIVE YOUR DAMN LIFE (CLUTTER FREE) 157

A note to anyone who's here because they loved *Tidy the F*ck Up*

First of all, thank you and welcome back! We covered a lot of ground in *Tidy the F*ck Up*, and it would suck for those of you who've read it to buy a second book just to get all the same info. Don't worry—I got you. *Nobody Wants Your Sh*t* is the next step in your decluttering evolution.

Death cleaning caters to those who are getting older and feel like their mortality is showing. So if you're old enough to complain about movie reboots, this book is for you. Sure, you may notice the occasional nod to *Tidy*'s real life–inspired decluttering tactics. (I'm not trying to reinvent the wheel here. If it works, it works.) But this sequel is all about your happily ever after.

Introduction

"Millions long for immortality who don't know what to do with themselves on a rainy Sunday afternoon." —Susan Ertz

You've tried marathon tidying, sparking joy, and putting everything in pretty bins. Now it's time to try a decluttering method that will help you get your shit together for once and for all: death cleaning. You may be asking yourself, "What in the depressing hell is 'death cleaning'?" Don't let the very stoic Swedish phrasing scare you—it's not as morbid as it sounds. In fact, it's pretty fucking empowering. You just made a face, didn't you? Just wait. Once you get the hang of this stuff, you'll be shocked by how much you like it.

Death cleaning, or *döstädning* in Swedish, is basically tidying like there's no tomorrow. But this isn't some sort of sadistic decluttering bootcamp. Statistically speaking, you're going to live (and continue to collect shit) for a really long time. And I know you've got more important things to do than organize your damn sock drawer.

Just think of death cleaning as a frame of mind that will light a fire under your messy ass when you need it. It helps you realize and accept that you don't have endless amounts of time to get your shit together, and that it's not going to get any easier the longer you put it off. Do you want to be sitting on the floor of your closet, cleaning out your Taylor Swift concert tees, when you're eighty years old and fresh off a knee replacement? No. You do not.

You also don't want to leave a clusterfuck for your loved ones to deal with after you're gone—*whenever* that may be. **They say clutter is nothing but delayed decisions. Delay long enough, and someone else will have to make those decisions.** (If that sounds like a good plan, you've got some work to do on you, my friend.) Do you want your memory to be a blessing to your friends and family, or do you want it to inspire hostility?

Maybe you live fifty more years, maybe you don't. But someday, it *will* be too late to get rid of those running shoes that you knew damn well you were never going to use. (It will also be too late to take up running, just FYI.) And if whoever inherits your shit is similarly disinclined to leave the couch, those shoes get added to a long, emotionally fraught to-do list. Not cool.

The bottom line is this: No one has as much time as they think they do. Not in a day, a year, or a lifetime. One way to deal with the existential dread that comes with that realization is to get your fucking ducks in a row. That means figuring out what makes you happy, ditching what doesn't, and putting shit where it belongs. It's not hard; it's just annoying. But it's also worth it. Not only will you have a clutter- and guilt-free space that feels amazing, you'll also learn to appreciate all those little things that make life worth living.

We human beings like to think we can control everything. Spoiler alert: we cannot. But taking control of our surroundings can easily scratch that itch. And it pays dividends for our mental health, physical health, and relationships. **An uncluttered space reduces anxiety and depression, helps you sleep better, curbs allergens, and boosts confidence.** Plus, it makes you a lot less likely to trip over your Chucks and break a fucking hip.

The trick isn't getting rid of your shit—it's letting go of your bullshit. If you've got stuff, you've got excuses to cling to it. And they're all valid. They're just not helpful.

You've picked up this book because some small, tucked-away part of you knows that. Or because you needed a laugh. Or maybe because your folks aren't getting any younger, and the sight of a lifetime's worth of crap stacked to the ceiling of their garage has unlocked a new level of anxiety you didn't know you had. Any which way, welcome! *Nobody Wants Your Sh*t* is going to be your new best friend—the kind that's smart, funny, supportive, and, most importantly, always calling you on your crap.

If you've read *Tidy the F*ck Up* (and you should— it's both helpful and hilarious), then you know that book was all about you. *Nobody Wants Your Sh*t* comes at organizing from a different angle. It's a take on death cleaning that helps you step outside your clutter bubble and imagine how your stuff will impact others, for better and for worse.

Let's be clear, though: that doesn't mean letting other people guilt you into making decisions you don't want to make or aren't ready to make. This is *your* shit, and as long as you're still north of the grass, you get to decide what happens to it. You're just going to take the long view when you do.

Whether you're tidying up or death cleaning, this decluttering stuff is all about figuring out what lights you up. Maybe it's keeping that ceramic frog collection until you're buried with it. Maybe it's gifting the little weirdos to your amphibian-obsessed niece to make her smile. Or maybe it's donating them to a thrift store so you don't have to dust the damn things anymore. **I've said it before, and I'll say it again: knowing what you want is a superpower.** Get clear on that, and everything else gets easier. Yep, even death.

Nobody Wants Your Sh*t

1

Why You Need
This Sh*t Now

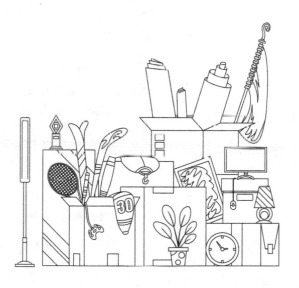

THE RIGHT HEADSPACE CHANGES EVERYTHING

Death cleaning isn't depressing—it's empowering as hell. (You'll see.) Downsizing, on the other hand, can be a real bitch. We usually associate it with hard times or old age, and it's almost always done out of grim necessity. But that's not death cleaning. If you confuse the two and come at this process thinking you have to get rid of all the things you love, and do it fast, you're not going to lift a pinky finger to do it. And I don't blame you. That sounds awful.

Death cleaning does *not* mean getting rid of your beloved belongings. All it asks you to do is weed out what's not working for you. The older you get, the more stuff you accumulate. Odds are, a lot of it isn't working for you anymore, and you know it. That's why you're here.

If you've read *Tidy the F*ck Up*, then you know the right perspective makes all the difference. In that book, I asked you to focus on what makes you happy and get rid of whatever brings you down. (Within reason. There's nothing exciting about a trash can, but you'd be pretty screwed without one.)

I maintain that, first and foremost, your home should be your happy place. Everything in it should light you up. Death cleaning invites you to go one step further. It makes you ask yourself not only "Does this make me happy?" but also "What happens to it when I'm gone?" And here's the good news: that type of thinking makes things even easier. All that stuff you're on the fence about? The stuff that makes you smile but doesn't really feel like you anymore? The stuff that you feel guilty getting rid of? When you think about it becoming a burden to someone else, ditching that stuff becomes a no-brainer. **We're here for a good time, not a long time.**

Maybe that stuffed animal your mom gave you makes you smile, but the grown-ass adult in you never knows quite what to do with it. When you realize that all your stuff is going to belong to someone else someday, it removes any lingering guilt. Gift that stuffie to your niece. You get to enjoy bringing a smile to her face *and* save someone else from feeling guilty about throwing Mr. McButtons in the trash in the future.

That's a win-win. You'll find there are a lot of those throughout this process. In fact, it's kind of the entire point of the process. By the end of it, you'll have a home that makes you happy *and* a clear conscience.

YOU'LL HAVE MORE TIME TO REAP THE BENEFITS

The whole idea behind death cleaning is dealing with your shit now so strangers and begrudging relatives don't have to do it later. But this isn't a completely altruistic process. The person who stands to gain the most from death cleaning is you. How, you ask? Let me count the scientifically proven ways:

1. **Better sleep and overall mental health**
2. **More energy and creativity**
3. **A deeper appreciation for what you have**

4. **More control over your life**

5. **Easier decisions**

6. **Clearer priorities**

7. **Less laundry**

8. **Fewer things to dust (and, therefore, fewer allergens)**

9. **Fewer arguments with loved ones**

10. **The ability to quickly find what you need**

11. **A connection to your space**

12. **A sense of accomplishment**

13. **More self-confidence**

14. **A clutter-free space you can be proud of**

15. **More time, room, and money for what you want**

So, basically, death cleaning makes life easier and you happier. (Plus, it gets you off your ass once in a while.) Not a bad trade-off for a bit of decluttering, now is it?

Pick whichever benefit calls to you like a siren to a seasick sailor and zero in on it. This is your why. Sure, you picked up this book for a reason. Maybe because you're starting to feel the too-rapid passage of time. Or maybe because, like me, you saw your parents' garage and started panicking about the too-rapid expansion of your own collection of miscellaneous crap. In other words, your reasons for death cleaning so far have been fear based. And fear is a damn good motivator. But it's not the best.

The best motivator is the one that makes you feel good. And that's entirely up to you. Is it not having to dust a dozen fucking mermaid figurines every week? Being able to pick out an outfit in under five minutes? A sense of having your shit together like a proper adult? Whatever your why is, really sit with it. **Imagine what it'll feel like when you've achieved your goal. That's the stuff of decluttering magic.** Come back to your why whenever you start to get sick of sorting. And you will get sick of it. But your why is going to keep you going—after your well-deserved break, that is.

If all you've got right now is fear, I get it. Decluttering feels like this massive, amorphous task on your already overwhelming to-do list. Don't worry, by the time we're done here, it'll feel like slathering on a mud mask and sipping a margarita. This is just stepped-up self-care.

For now, try to flip that fear on its head. You know that feeling of panic you get when the doorbell rings? It's because you know your house looks like shit, and you're worried someone's going to see it. Instead of focusing on the anxiety caused by your mother-in-law popping by for a surprise inspection—I mean, *visit*—focus on what you have to gain. How great would it be if you didn't have to worry because you always had your fucking ducks in a row? There's your why. Wield that happy feeling like Harry Potter and his badass, Dementor-busting Patronus.

LIVING IN PEACE IS BETTER THAN RESTING IN PEACE

If you watch the news, scroll through social media, or, really, are alive in any way, you know that the world is a crazy, nerve-wracking place. Earthquakes, floods, famine, violence, fires, wars—we all need a fucking break now and then.* First and foremost, we can be grateful to have a roof over our heads and the luxury of needing to pare down. And with that gratitude in mind, we can turn our homes into a quiet respite from the rest of the world.

What that looks like is going to depend on what floats your particular boat. What says "sanctuary" to you? Is it piles of crap and clutter everywhere you look? Probably not. Maybe it's space to roll out the ol' yoga mat without being encumbered by a pile of dog toys. Maybe it's an ergonomic gaming chair and a beautifully organized collection of action-adventure RPGs. **Whatever mental image helps your shoulders relax and disconnect from your ears, you can make it your reality. You just need to put in the work. And if you start now, you'll have plenty of time to enjoy it.**

****Bonus:** Having your shit together can really help you in an emergency. Not only will you know where stuff is when you need it, you'll also know what's important enough to you to grab on your way out the door. In this unpredictable world of ours, that's a big plus (even if the thought does make you want to eat whipped cream straight from the can while in the fetal position).

After all, life is supposed to get easier, less stressful, and more comfortable as you get older. (I said *supposed to*.) You want to be able to kick back before you kick the bucket, right? Not spend your golden years fruitlessly searching through overstuffed drawers for the arthritis cream until you keel over and your kids have to deal with your mess? Doesn't sound as fun as relaxing in the home library you created in what used to be your junk room, does it? No, it does not.

The bottom line is, your house isn't a fucking storage unit, and you're not just waiting around to die. You're living. In your home. So why not make the most of the time and the space you have while you have it?

IT'S NOT GOING TO GET ANY EASIER WHILE YOU KEEP ACCUMULATING CRAP

Look around. How much stuff do you have right now compared with ten years ago? How much more stuff do you think you'll have ten years from now? If you're reading this, odds are your possessions are multiplying as quickly as the dust bunnies that cling to them. The question is, what happens next?

Do you decide that it's Future You's problem and let the clutter continue unabated? No. **A home that's overflowing with stuff doesn't just exact a mental and emotional toll. It's physically taxing.** And none of us is getting any younger. Maybe you're one of those people who's in the best shape of their life when they turn sixty, and you can keep lugging those seasonal decorations down from the attic without a second thought. More likely, Future You hurts your back if you so much as dare to get off the couch. You're either going to slow down or run out of fucks as you get older. Probably both. So the time to minimize how often you need to climb that damn ladder is now.

Decluttering is one of those things you have to do for the rest of your life. But you get to decide whether it's a matter of ditching a newly worn-out tee shirt or renting a dumpster. Every day you put it off, the problem grows like a marshmallow in the microwave, threatening to explode into a mess that outright *demands* your attention. Not super comforting, I know. But if you start now, it all gets a hell of a lot easier from here. So take the marshmallow out of the microwave and just fucking eat it.

YOU'RE NEVER GOING TO "GET AROUND TO IT"

What percentage of things that you said you'd "get around to" have you actually gotten around to? The sink still drips, your junk drawer has become a junk closet, and you've given up entirely on putting away your laundry. That basket is an honorary drawer now. You're not going to *get around to* decluttering. If you have any free time at all, you'll get around to sitting on your ass and watching three hours of *The Office* before you so much as sort your socks.

And that's completely fair. You're exhausted! We all are. **Life gets in the way of so many of our good intentions. But if you want a clutter-free house, you have to**

make it a priority. If you don't, you're going to keep tripping over piles of clothes for the rest of your life (which could be considerably shorter if you're tripping over stuff all the time). So suck it up, buttercup, and get to work!

As for watching your comfort shows instead of sorting? The real decluttering pros do both. Turn the TV on and your brain off, and check some of those annoyingly monotonous to-dos off your list. You can toss worn-out socks and underwear, sort stacks of mail for recycling, or clear old files off your computer in less time than it takes to watch an episode. **Get creative with your decluttering, and you can find ways to make it work for you.**

YOU CAN'T DIE UNTIL YOU CLEAN OUT YOUR GARAGE

Whenever my dad starts talking about final arrangements, I tell him he's not allowed to die until he cleans out his garage. If you saw his garage, you'd understand. The man has never met a curbside freebie he didn't think he would fix up and use someday. (To his credit, he's upcycled a fair amount of stuff.) And I'm not about to go through that mess with a fine-tooth comb. I gave him fair warning: deal with it yourself, or else the minute you're gone, I open the doors and put up a "free to good home" sign.

Dad appreciates smart-assed tough love. (Where do you think I get it from?) He took the challenge and ran with it, cleaning a bunch of crap out of both the house and the garage. And then, just as quickly, he filled both back up. Apparently, he missed the part about changing your clutter-clutching ways after the cleanup. That part's important. The point is to end up with fewer things than you started with.

You do not have endless amounts of time to deal with the massive amount of stuff you've accumulated in your life—especially if you continue to accumulate it. At some point, it's game over. And while you may find comfort in having a floor-to-ceiling chest of tiny drawers that hold every kind of nut, bolt, and nail in existence, I promise you that your kids will not share your appreciation for it. Keep what you need (*actually* need, not *might* need) and what you love, and let the rest go to good homes of your choosing.* Then stop. Bringing. Shit. Home. If you leave it until it's too late, you don't get a vote in where things end up.

NO ONE HAS TIME TO DEAL WITH YOUR SHIT

You don't know what busy looks like until you have to take time off work and out of your life to clean up someone else's estate. It's a hell of a lot more complex than decluttering your own stuff. Not only do you have to deal with all the paperwork and planning that comes with final arrangements, you also have to clear out a loved one's belongings while grieving them. And you usually have a finite amount of time to get it all done.

---

*It's okay if one of those "good homes" is the trash. Not everything is worth saving or donating. More on that later.

Do you really want to lay all of that responsibility on someone else because you couldn't find five minutes a day to sort through a drawer? No, because you're not a monster. **You're just overwhelmed. But if you start now, you have plenty of time to get the job done and revel in the rewards of having your shit together.**

You can declutter a few minutes at a time, or you can spend weekends here and there doing your best impression of the Tasmanian Devil. Whichever you choose, you get to do it without pressure, guilt, grief, and resentment. That's not to say you won't feel some feelings while decluttering—it can be an emotional process. But it's nothing compared to death cleaning for someone who's actually, you know, dead.

FORGET DYING— MOVING REALLY SUCKS

Think you're busy now? Try decluttering when you're up against an expensive clock. When you add a move to the mix, you're really going to start regretting your life choices. But you don't have the physical flexibility to deal with a lifetime's worth of stuff and kick yourself at the same time.

Whether you move for work, downsize as you get older, retire abroad, or just feel like a change of scenery, odds are pretty good that you're going to move at least one more time before you die. **You don't want to lay out an extra rent or mortgage payment because you didn't have your shit together.** Moving usually means decluttering, cleaning, and packing in just a few weeks. And no one wants to spend all their free time (or their PTO, for that matter) doing all that when they could have been kicking back on a beach somewhere instead.

The more stuff you have, the more of a pain in the ass it is to move. And if you're downsizing, you need to be even more decisive about what goes with you because it literally won't all fit. Make sure you've measured the new space and all the furniture you hope to move into it. You don't want your TV stand ending up on the curb on moving day because you couldn't squeeze it into your new living room.

Take a minute right now to look around at all your stuff and imagine what it'll be like to get ready for a move. Got it? It will be *infinitely* worse than that. Moving is like giving birth—you always underestimate how hard it's going to be. A year or two afterward, you're so focused on your new life that you forget that the process of getting there was painful as fuck.

The difference is that moving doesn't have to be painful. You can make it ten times easier if you start decluttering—let me hear you say it—*now*. After all, do you want to do it at your own pace while enjoying a true-crime podcast? Or do you want to be frantically throwing shit in unmarked boxes while paying movers to sit back and enjoy a sandwich? It's entirely up to you, but I'd pick Door #1.

GRIEVING IS HARD ENOUGH

When you die, do you want your kids to reminisce about all the great times you had together? Or do you want them sorting through a lifetime's worth of crap and cursing your name? (I mean, that's one way to help them get over your death quickly.)

Those are the two paths you get to choose from. And it is a choice—your choice. You can thoughtfully declutter your home over the years, gifting meaningful items to friends and family as you go and seeing the joy these special gifts bring them. Or you can continue to amass a personal collection of things that will challenge the patience and sanity of whoever has to deal with them when you're gone. Quite the legacy that would be! Remember that the next time you decide to bring home another box of yard-sale finds.

No one wants to declutter while they're grieving, but we're all going to have to do it at some point or another. The least we can do is put ourselves in the

shoes of those who have to do it for us. They'll have enough on their plates without having to decide which model trains to keep. Plus, no one has enough PTO to clean out a clusterfuck of a house in one go, which means it will be an exhausting burden to them for months.

Imagine that it's your parent or your partner. Those memory-infused items will now seem like all you have left of the person you loved. **But a thing is not a memory. It's just a thing.** Knowing what was truly important to them and what wasn't helps you grieve for the person without grieving for their stuff. That's the gift you have the power to give your loved ones.

Go through the process now, together, so you don't have to face it alone later. (Unless getting your partner to part with their library bargain books is like pulling teeth. Then you might have to be a little more strategic about their involvement.)

Chapter 1 Checklist

- [ ] Focus on making your home your happy place
- [ ] Remember that the benefits of death cleaning outweigh the annoyances
- [ ] Create a home that reduces your stress instead of making it worse
- [ ] Face the fact that you're not getting any younger
- [ ] Suck it up like the grown-ass adult you are and stop procrastinating
- [ ] Realize that you're up against a deadline (so to speak)
- [ ] Start now so that you can enjoy the rewards for years to come
- [ ] Save money, time, and brain cells by paring down before you're forced to
- [ ] Choose how you want to be remembered

2

Stop Buying Into Your Own Bullsh*t

YOUR EXCUSES ARE TRASH

You know you have too much shit—that's a given. And you know you have to do something about it. Why else would you have picked up a book about decluttering? But you didn't pick up just any book. You picked up *this* book. You're here for the real talk, the tough love, the scoop. You want to know why you do what you do and how to stop doing it. In other words, you're here to have someone call you on your bullshit.

So why haven't you done anything about your clusterfuck of a clutter situation? Maybe you've tried and gotten two pairs of shoes in before calling it quits. (Valiant effort. Try again.) Maybe you don't know where to start. (This one's not complicated—start literally anywhere, with anything. Just start. Then keep doing it. This goes for anything you want to do.) Or maybe, and most likely, you're talking yourself out of it on a daily basis.

That's the human condition—constantly inventing reasons not to do the thing we know we need to do. That's why we drink coffee instead of water, eat junk food too often, and hold onto old versions of ourselves long after we've outgrown them. It's easier than doing the work on ourselves and our spaces. And it's one of the biggest obstacles we face when it comes to death cleaning. You're older now, so that shit is entrenched.

Next time you find yourself making excuses not to declutter, explore them. What lies are you telling yourself today? If a friend came at you with the same bullshit excuses, what would you say to them?

Calling yourself on your bullshit is the only way to power through it. Once you're on the other side, you'll wonder why you wasted so much energy lying to yourself about how many shoes you really need. (Don't even argue—I know you have too damn many pairs of shoes.)

WHICH EXCUSE SOUNDS LIKE YOU?
No, you're not going to need it someday

I am the queen of buying stuff for a single purpose and then holding onto it forever in case I need it. Hoisin sauce for a recipe that's too much work to make again, an air mattress from the first and last time I went camping, a truly insane amount of gift wrap for every possible occasion, and so on and so on. So I speak from experience when I say: use it, or lose it.

And when I say "use it," I mean immediately. If you haven't found a use for the thing within two weeks of actively trying to find one, you're not going to. What's the worst that will happen if you get rid of it and then need it in the future? You bought it once; you can always buy it again. Is it wasteful? Maybe. But it's more wasteful to have shit you're not using taking up space you could be using for something you actually want or need. **The stuff you own should be earning its keep.**

Worse than keeping things in case you need them is keeping things in case someone else needs them.

This one's for anyone who saw "air mattress" and thought "keep for guests." I'm going to need you to read that last paragraph again. There's no difference between keeping that air mattress in case you ever attempt camping again and keeping it in case you have extra guests when you have a guest room or a perfectly good couch. And there's definitely no point in keeping it if the last time you hosted an overnight guest was at some sort of childhood slumber party. **Nothing should take up valuable space 100 percent of the time for a .001 percent chance you'll need it.**

Beyond a clean blanket, pillow, and towel—all of which should be in regular rotation at your house anyway—you can count on your guests to bring what they need. If they don't, they can hit up the nearest drugstore like a normal person. You're not running a fucking Airbnb. And as someone who loves a good mini-toiletry section, I think there are worse things in life than needing to buy a tiny bottle of contact solution.

If you, too, like a good mini-toiletry section and have basically established one in your home, use them up *now*. Beauty samples, too. (I see you, beauty-box subscribers.) The damn things don't keep forever. And I reiterate: unless your house is an Airbnb, you shouldn't have a basket full of tiny shampoos and toothpastes. When you need them for a trip, buy new ones and then use *them* up. Better yet, invest in reusable travel bottles you can refill from your regular products like the sustainability-minded person you are. Win-win.

Dishes are meant to be used, not displayed

Do you have gorgeous, gilded table settings for twelve stuck in a hutch next to a table for six that's covered in mail and laundry? Although every HGTV show features a couple who makes seven figures milking geese and loves to entertain over wine and charcuterie, most people are busy and eat a good percentage of their meals in front of the television. It's okay if life isn't as elegant as you imagined. **Happy beats the hell out of elegant.**

If it makes you happy to see your dishes proudly displayed like they are in the imaginary kitchens of cooking shows and dream of elegant dinner parties to come, great. No changes needed. But if you don't notice those dishes until there's a thick coat of dust on the hutch—or worse, you feel a pang of guilt or remorse when you look at them—it's time to make a change.

Maybe you sell the dishes *and* the hutch and buy yourself a coffee table with a lift top so you don't have to balance takeout on your lap. Or maybe you decide to use the dishes and add a touch of elegance to every meal, takeout or not. And if it's just that your days of entertaining are behind you, maybe you gift the dishes to someone who will love them as much as you have. Whatever you do, find a way to make those dishes work.

Obviously, I'm not just talking about dishes here. Everything we buy, we buy for the life we imagine for ourselves—an armchair, a pair of sneakers, a killer gaming system—whatever. **The point is to look at each item you own and determine whether it's living up to its potential *now*.** Maybe it fit into your life when you bought it, and now it doesn't. Or maybe you hoped it would, and it hasn't. But if you don't look at it and feel excited about the next time you'll get to use it, it's not doing you a damn bit of good physically, mentally, or emotionally. It's just taking up space.

You have time to watch bad TV

In American culture, our worth as human beings often gets tied up in how busy and productive we are. So we pack our schedules to the brim until our default setting becomes "I don't have time for that." Talk about bull-shit. **First of all, we don't have to do a damn thing to be of value. And second, we find time for the things that are important to us.** If you've picked up this book, getting your shit together is somewhere on that list. Time to move it to the top.

Don't get me wrong—you are absolutely entitled to sit on your ass, eating Goldfish crackers and watching *Real Housewives*. This world is *a lot*, and it'd be a hell of a lot better if we all took the time we need to decompress. But if you have time to watch the live creation of internet memes, you have time to declutter. And between the two, a clutter-free space is probably better for your mental health in the long run.

If you really can't imagine how you're going to squeeze all this death cleaning into your schedule, you're thinking too big. You're not going to be cleaning out the closet on day one. And if you think you have to, you're going to avoid the hell out of it. **The trick is to start so small that you can't possibly talk yourself out of it.**

Try decluttering for just five minutes a day at first. Five minutes of putting shit where it belongs, or of finding one thing you know you can live without. Write "donate" on a box and spend a few minutes a day adding to it. Write it in your planner, set an alarm on your phone, or tell the nearest digital assistant to remind you to do it at a particular time each day. **In other words, stop overthinking it and just start doing it.** Once you build some momentum and start seeing results, you'll be surprised by how much time you find to get the job done.

Guilt is for suckers

How much stuff are you holding onto because you feel too guilty to get rid of it? The answer is too fucking much. If you never felt any guilt, I'd be worried. That and eating a burrito like it's corn on the cob are the hallmarks of a psychopath.

A little guilt is natural. But so is a strong desire not to go to work. Sometimes you have to move through these feelings to get what you need (like a paycheck). And you need a house that isn't bursting at the seams with stuff that makes you say "ugh" or makes your heirs want to spit on your grave.

You can appreciate something and still not want it around. That sweater from your dad was so thoughtful (however terribly misguided).* You got a lot of use out of those pots and pans before you upgraded. That teddy bear from your childhood was well loved. **Hold onto the gratitude—that's the important part—and let**

---

*Hot tip: Most gift givers won't remember what they got you after a few months. So stop reminding them by breaking it out when they visit. If Dad happens to ask, that sweater is in the laundry because you just wore it.

the thing go. Someone else is going to love it.

However, when you've loved something so well that it doesn't work anymore or looks like hell, it doesn't get donated. It goes in the trash. If you're anything like me (and you probably are if you're feeling guilty about getting rid of inanimate objects), that one hurts. But it's going to end up there any which way. And we're not passing the buck anymore, remember? That's the whole fucking point of this. **The thing served its purpose. Take a moment to feel grateful, then move on.**

Your sanity is more important than the money you spent

Ever look at something you know you don't actually want, need, or use that's taking up perfectly good space in your house and immediately think, *but I spent good money on that*? Me too. And I'm here to tell you, that's not a reason to keep it.

This is just another incarnation of guilt, and we're not playing its little games anymore. Instead of thinking about how much money you spent on that stiff leather jacket you never wear, think of getting rid of it as investing in your sanity. **Study after study shows that a clean, clutter-free space pays dividends for your mental health.** You might live another fifty years. Do you want to live it with your buyer's remorse staring you in the face every time you open your closet? Worse, do you want someone thinking that this thing meant the world to you and feeling like they have to keep it too? After all, you cared about it enough to hang onto it. Right?

You see where I'm going with this. **We keep the stuff that's important to us. Everything else goes. Period.** If you'd bought that jacket at a yard sale for a dollar, that uncomfortable fucker would be in the trash by now. Consider it the price of a masterclass in not buying shit you don't need. Worth every penny.

There's more than one way to jog a memory

Say it with me now: A thing is not a memory. It's just a thing. If you can remember the joy of driving your first car without the damn thing rusting in your garage, you can remember the way your baby daughter looked in her pink gingham dress without keeping it in mothballs in your attic.

Saving that dress for your daughter's daughter? I've got some bad news for you: she probably doesn't want it. Not only does it smell like mothballs, it also screams nineties and has a suspicious stain on the back. If you're saving it just for the memory, then I'm not sure you know how memories work.

Your need to hold onto things was always about the feelings those things inspired. The things themselves are just conduits. So hold onto the feelings and throw the musty old dress in the trash.* Your

---

* Obviously, this doesn't apply to heirloom pieces in good condition. Those you can donate or sell when your kid tells you they don't want them.

daughter had the dress when she needed it, and you have the happy memory (and probably more than a few photos). Be grateful without being maudlin.

If you really need the visual, take a quick pic with your phone before decluttering something senti-mental. Create a "memories" folder on your phone and get nostalgic whenever the mood strikes. Or whenever your photos app decides to trigger you with surprise slideshows. That's always fun.

That stuff belonged to the old you

We collect stuff for every stage of our lives, but we don't declutter at the same pace. It's not just laziness (although that's definitely a big part of it). And it's not just that you get busier as you get older (although you definitely do). It's how you see your stuff.

We hold onto things that reflect who we are, even long after we've outgrown them physically and emotionally. Not all clutter is created equal. You might feel a little nostalgic for the old IKEA furniture from your first apartment, but that's not stopping you from upgrading when you get the chance. So what makes that different than, say, getting rid of your prom dress? You can still see yourself reflected in the dress but not in the furniture.

Big life changes—like the promotion that affords you the new furniture or the move that necessitates it— tend to shake us out of our clutter-filled reverie. That IKEA dresser belonged to the old you . . . the broke you you're happy to see the back of. The new furniture reflects who you are now. But most transitions in life are more subtle. When you're eighty, you'll still feel like your eighteen-year-old self, twirling around in that dress. (Mentally. Physically, you are painfully aware that eighteen was a long fucking time ago.)

It helps that you don't have room for two dining-room tables. (If you get new stuff and put the old stuff in storage, that's a whole other problem. I'll see you on page 98.) Maybe you can't actually fit into that prom dress anymore—or, more likely, you wouldn't want to— but the dress still fits in your closet. So you rationalize keeping it when you damn well know it should have been out the door decades ago. **It's time to let go of who you used to be and embrace who you are now.**

Maybe yoga used to be your thing, but now MMA fighting is more your style. As you embrace the new you, you can probably gift the meditation cushion to a more Zen-minded friend. Maybe you've kept your kids' rooms intact, but you're an empty nester who's ready for some proper guest rooms. Give those freeloaders a firm deadline to come get their shit before it hits the donate pile. **Our priorities change as we get older. The things we surround ourselves with need to change with them.** You're not the person you were in 1998. (Thank God. Low-rise jeans were the worst.)

It's not a damn security blanket

There are a lot of reasons we hold onto shit we don't need, but one of the most pernicious is the comfort we get from being surrounded by all of it. We chose this stuff piece by piece. It represents parts of us and the life we've lived. How can we get rid of it? And what if we never find another pair of jeans that fit like this one? Never mind the fact that there are holes in the thighs and they haven't fit in three fucking years. They're so comfy!

See that? That's called rationalization. You're justifying holding onto something when you know damn well you should get rid of it. Stop doing that. **Stop holding onto shit that no longer serves you.** You will find another pair of really great jeans. It might take a while, but you will. And that will give you enough time to learn your fucking lesson and buy an extra pair this time. (Really great jeans are hard to find and don't last forever, so as long as they're in good shape—I repeat, *in good shape*—they get a pass on the decluttering.)

At some point, you have to face the fact that the anxiety your clutter is causing you vastly outweighs any comfort you derive from it. You know what's more comforting than a basement packed with decades' worth of bins, boxes, and worn-out jeans? A home theater. Or a home gym, I guess, if that's your thing. Or just open fucking space.

You might have an especially hard time with this

one if you've experienced financial hardship. Maybe you hold on tight to everything you have because there was a time when you didn't have enough. Or you're afraid to replace items because you might need the money for other things. That's called a scarcity mindset, and it's completely valid. But it's definitely not helpful when you're trying to declutter. If you're ready to work through it, friends, family, and/or a qualified professional can help.

There's nothing comforting about clutter caving in on you from every side. But coming home to a clean, decluttered space where the things you really love have the space to shine? Now *that's* comforting. So make room for change. Make room for happiness. Make room for that home theater! Or the gym thing. Whatever.

There's nothing homey about a house full of junk

No one's saying that your home should look like a page out of *Architectural Digest*. It's supposed to look lived in. You live there. That means there's a good amount of stuff in it that reflects who you are and how you live. But there is a happy medium to be had here—a home that reflects who you are while giving you room to breathe. That's the sweet spot we're working toward.

Come back to your why for a minute. What's your endgame? **Go around your home and imagine what each space will look like after you've met that goal. How does the space feel?** Lighter? Calming? Functional? *Homey*? If it doesn't, adjust your goal. It's supposed to make you feel good, remember?

Now, if you *want* your home to look like a page out of *AD*, go for it. Rock that elegant minimalism. Or go full *HGTV* with the quirky finishes and cowhide rugs. Whatever floats your stylishly decorated boat. The point is to take control of the situation. This is your home. You get to decide what it looks like. But that means actually being intentional about what stays and what goes until it feels homey to you. And staying the hell away from the shops in the meantime. You do not need one more fucking candle.

You're not the only one who thinks it's a pain in the ass

Human beings are lazy as hell. But give us a simple task that requires both physical effort *and* emotional gymnastics, and we'd rather do the obstacle course from *American Ninja Warrior*. We will jump through literal fucking hoops before doing any sort of work on ourselves.

We want the easy solution, the quick fix. But there's no quick fix for decluttering a lifetime's worth of furniture, clothing, memories, and miscellaneous crap. Well, there is, but it involves bulldozers and dumpsters and usually some kind of biohazard warning. That's not how you want this to go down.

The longer you've let shit pile up, the harder it's

going to be to deal with. That's on you. Did you really think you'd just keep buying stuff and never have to get rid of anything? Just curious . . . how did you think this would end? Your mourners would come to collect everything, clutching your ugly-hat collection to their chests? Or someone would set up an estate sale for your Aerosmith fan tees? The bulldozer's more likely.

No one wants to deal with your crap any more than you do. Nor should they have to. This is literally your mess. You clean it up. The good news is no one is saying you have to do it all at once. Take it one day at a time, but start now. Like, right now. Put the book down and find one thing to declutter—a drawer full of soy sauce packets, your key ring collection, that pair of underwear you keep saying you're going to throw out. Do it. Throw the fuckers out. I'll wait.

How good did that feel? Imagine how accomplished you'll feel after doing a closet or room. That's the good shit, and it makes the work worth it. Well, that and knowing you're not going to be a burden to others. That's good too.

Relief beats regret every day of the week

Worried that you'll regret unloading those vintage Corelle dishes and run back to the thrift store, desperation in your eyes, only to find they've sold? Not gonna happen. First of all, things are not vintage just because they're old. "Vintage" implies age *and* value. Those dishes are old. Second of all, they didn't grow legs and walk themselves to Goodwill. You tossed them for a reason.* When in doubt, always come back to your why.

The percentage of things you'll regret tossing is absolutely dwarfed by the relief you'll feel every time you unload something you don't need and free up space in your home. But definitely check pockets, containers, and drawers before you donate anything. You're not going to regret donating old clothes, but you might be sad to lose that crumpled twenty you left in your coat pocket.

If you do happen to miss an object you've donated, just imagine how happy it will make someone else.

---

*Disclaimer: If that reason didn't come from a deep-seated why (see chapter 1), you might regret your choice. Don't let anyone guilt you into getting rid of your shit just for the sake of getting rid of it. You have to want this.

Those Corelle dishes served you well, and now they'll serve someone else well, because Corelle is fucking indestructible. And someone out there will be thrilled to complete their set of Abundance bowls. You've given your stuff a second chance and given someone else the opportunity to make new memories around it. How awesome are you? Really awesome. (And if you *really* miss it, there's this little thing called the internet. You can probably buy it again. But you didn't hear that from me.)

"Wasteful" is holding onto shit you don't use

If you're someone who hates to be wasteful, death cleaning can feel especially pushy. This isn't ordinary decluttering, where you might justify holding onto that toaster long after it's outlived its usefulness. The bar is higher now.

Every item needs to earn its keep. Does it make you happy? Do you use it? Does it fit into your life? If you're on the fence, it's out the door. I don't care if the toaster has a frozen-foods button. (But seriously, where has that been all our lives?) It's been in a cabinet since you got the air fryer. Out it goes.

Getting rid of shit you don't want, need, or use isn't wasteful. Letting it take up space in your home or keeping it when someone else could be using it is. You paid good money for it? You paid good money for your home. Try doing the math sometime: the cost of your home divided by its square footage. That's how much each square foot is costing you. Is that toaster worth the space it's taking up now? Didn't think so.

I get it—few things feel worse than throwing away your stuff. It might be junk, but it's *your* junk. And there are a whole bunch of psychological reasons for that attachment. But keeping that junk isn't doing you any good. Luckily, the trash isn't your only option. **Most stuff can be recycled, upcycled, sold, donated, or gifted. Find the solution that works for you.** But don't let that toaster stay in your house for one more fucking minute.

By taking a tiny bit of extra time to find a new home for something you don't need anymore, you're giving it a chance to find the person who needs it most in that moment. As opposed to, you know, foisting your shit on a friend or family member who risks breaking a tooth from clenching their jaw when they thank you for it. That's another death-cleaning win-win.

Your color-coordinated storage bins are bullshit

Organizing your clutter is not the same thing as decluttering. And throwing shit in bins isn't either. Sure, it looks nicer. But the relief you feel at seeing all that stuff neatly hidden away is just another clue that it's irking you and needs to be dealt with.

Let's say you have stacks and stacks of color-coordinated tees, sweaters, and pants in those plastic dividers. Everything's in its place, and It's easy to see what you have and find what you need. You're done, right? Wrong. You still have stacks and stacks of clothing—much of which you probably don't wear—taking up space in your home. Rationalize it all you want with your little dividers, but those copious stacks are making you anxious. Plus, pulling out a tee involves Jenga-like skill and possibly a minor meltdown.

Picture instead a beautifully curated collection of your favorite clothing and accessories. You wear all of it. And you have so much room in your closet that each item has breathing room around it, so you can see and grab everything easily. You can't tell me that doesn't sound like a massive improvement. **Decluttering comes first. Organization, second. Don't organize a damn thing until you decide what items have earned a place in your home.**

ONE MAN'S TRASH IS ANOTHER UNRELATED MAN'S TREASURE

Do you have Great-Grandma Mary's flower-adorned dishes delicately stored in boxes to give to your kids when they get married? Or cute little outfits and squishy stuffed animals tucked away for grandkids you don't yet have? Are you picturing passing down your love of fixing up old cars, complete with your favorite socket-wrench set?

You know what they say about assuming, right? And those are some pretty presumptuous assumptions. Hate to break it to you, but fewer people are getting married and having kids these days. And there's no guarantee that yours are going to like what you like. **That's why you need to check in with your loved ones regularly and make sure you're on the same page about anything you're thinking of bequeathing to them.** If you know you're only getting a grandpuppy, you can swap those baby clothes out for a monogrammed leash set that's sure to garner more appreciation.

The idea of leaving something that's important to you behind for the next generation is sweet but woefully misguided. That thing is important to *you*. There's no guarantee that it's going to be important to your family. They certainly don't want to be guilted into keeping it because you left it to them on your deathbed. **Instead of willing things away like a mysterious great-uncle, talk to your family now.**

It's better to know now that your shit is headed for the thrift store instead of your daughter's house when you die. Save both of you some trouble by taking it there now. (As long as you're no longer using it and ready to part with it. After all, this is your life and you're still very much living it.) The stuff that's important to you might not be important to anyone related to you, but someone out there is going to love it. And they'll love it more because it doesn't smack of familial guilt or resentment.

YOU WON'T MISS WHAT YOU HAVEN'T LAID EYES ON IN YEARS

This one's actually kind of a lie. When you open up a box full of stuff you haven't seen in two years, what's the first thing you do? You exclaim, "Oh, I forgot about this!" Suddenly you can't live without it—even though you put it in that box because you decided you *could* live without it, and you have successfully lived without it for two years.

When it comes to our crap, we seem to adhere to two contrasting clichés simultaneously: "out of sight, out of mind" and "absence makes the heart grow fonder." When you open the box, you suddenly miss what you didn't remember existed five minutes ago. It's new and nostalgic all at once.

That box is the Schrödinger's cat of personal belongings. It's both wanted and unwanted, junk and prized possession. When you filled it, you were sure everything in it was bound for the thrift store. But you didn't take it to the thrift store, did you? You threw it in the basement or drove around with it in the trunk of your car, *just in case*. Keep it closed, and it's surplus crap. Open it, and you start rethinking all your life choices.

Do not second-guess your decluttering decisions. You're a smart cookie. You took your time, weighed your options, made informed decisions. Or you said "fuck it" and went with your gut. Either way, trust yourself. And don't open the damn box. You've lived this long without whatever's in that box. Drop it off at the thrift store and go about your happy, clutter-free life.

If you completely ignore my advice, open the box, and suddenly can't live without its contents, you better put them to good use. Do not just leave them in the fucking box. Donate other things to make room for them, or rotate like items to keep everything feeling fresh—whatever you've got to do to keep your space clutter-free.* And let your loved ones know that it's straight to the fucking thrift store after you're gone.

YOU ONLY THINK YOU'RE HAPPY LIVING THIS WAY

You think you're in control here. But the truth is, at some point, your stuff took over. That's what happens when you keep adding and adding without subtracting, curating, or being intentional about what makes its way

---

*The same goes for toys. Cats, dogs, and kids will be thrilled to see their old friends again when you covertly rotate them in and others out. (If you don't love that your behavior mirrors your dog's, maybe drop that fucking box off at the thrift store already.)

into your home. It's time to pump the fucking brakes and remember who's driving this thing. And that starts with seeing what you have—*really* seeing it.

You've probably gotten so used to most of your stuff that you don't even notice it anymore. When's the last time you looked at the art on your walls? Or the photos you've framed? Or the books that line your shelves? Not just to dust them, but to appreciate them. When you declutter, you're forced to bring your undivided attention to each object. Therein lies an opportunity.

We've already covered the many benefits of getting your shit together. But there's one more that you may have noticed along the way, and it's a big one: gratitude. **When you take the time to sit with all of things you own, you develop a deeper appreciation for them, for the memories they helped create, and for how far you've come.**

That closer look can also help you decide that something has served its purpose, like those beach chairs you used constantly in Maine but haven't seen since moving to Wisconsin. Or help you notice that something needs a little more love than you've given it, like that half-dead succulent by the window. (Go water the damn thing.)

As you investigate each object, you'll find yourself feeling more and more grateful for a life well lived. You don't need to hold onto your stuff to hold onto that feeling. **By decluttering from a place of appreciation, you free yourself from the hold your stuff has over you.** Now, living firmly in the present, you start to create your happy place. (Hint: It probably doesn't include Grandpa's sad clown art. Your kids will thank you to throw that shit out.)

Chapter 2 Checklist

- ☐ **Stop making excuses and get to fucking work**
- ☐ **Make sure everything you own is earning its keep—housing is expensive as hell**
- ☐ **Focus on making the most of the life you actually have, not the one you imagined**
- ☐ **Stop overthinking it and just start doing it a few minutes a day**

- [ ] Hold onto your memories and let the thing go

- [ ] Worry more about your mental health than the money you spent

- [ ] Let go of who you used to be and embrace the badass you are now

- [ ] Stop holding onto shit that isn't working for you

- [ ] Imagine how you want your space to feel, not how you want it to look

- [ ] Remember why you're doing this shit

- [ ] Take responsibility for your own fucking mess

- [ ] Check pockets and drawers before making donations, then let that shit go

- [ ] Talk to your loved ones before you hoard stuff they don't want

- [ ] Stop letting things waste away in your home when they could be doing someone else some good

- [ ] Focus on finding the right home for your stuff rather than foisting it on relatives

- [ ] Don't organize a damn thing until you've decluttered it completely

- [ ] Don't second-guess yourself

- [ ] Appreciate what your stuff says about how far you've come

3
Simplify Your F*cking Life

DECIDE TO GO ALL—IN ON GETTING YOUR SH*T TOGETHER

Your mentality plays a huge role in how successful you are at anything you do, so it shouldn't be a shock to discover that decluttering is no exception. But the overwhelm is real. You can't be guilted or bullied into getting your shit together. It won't stick. You'll just get more and more resentful with every box you take out of your home.

Your motivation has to come from deep inside you. That's where your why comes in. If none of the reasons listed in chapter 1 are doing it for you, come up with your own. Or take this one from *Tidy the F*ck Up*: You're so sick of your own bullshit that you can't stand it anymore, and you're ready to make a change. Once you're clear on your why, declare it to the world. Or to your cat. Whatever makes it feel official to you.

Fully committing to getting your shit together once and for all is the only way to get the job done. That doesn't mean working around the clock or paring down to the bare minimum, though. Those are just quick ways to piss you off and make sure you don't want to declutter so much as a pencil cup. All-or-nothing approaches don't work.

When you decide to cut back on sugar, do you throw out all your Oreos? No, because three hours later you're buying a pack at the gas station and eating them in the car.* Tackle that Oreo habit with mindfulness and moderation, though, and you might get some traction. Same with decluttering.

Going all-in just means deciding to do the damn thing. In your mind, you're ready, willing, and able to get your shit together. You're going to make a plan and follow through—no more excuses. But we're aiming for progress here, not perfection. Why? Because perfection is bullshit. It's not attainable. So we're not going to waste our fucking time on it.

Taking the tiniest of baby steps? Imagining how you want your home to feel? Doing a few minutes a

---

*I have never personally tried to give up sugar, because chocolate, but I have heard tell.

day to get your bearings? That's the good stuff. Keep
going. **Just decide you're done fucking around and
hold yourself accountable to that.**

IMAGINE CREATING A SPACE YOU CAN'T GET ENOUGH OF

Yes, death cleaning is about decluttering for whoever
has to deal with your shit when you're gone. But you're
not dead yet. In the meantime, you deserve a home
that makes you happy. (I'm assuming. But maybe
you're the kind of person who doesn't put their shopping cart back in the rack. In which case, my car and
I wish you all the pointy coffee tables.) So "happy" is
your starting point.

Anyone who says money can't buy happiness has
obviously never strolled through a TJ Maxx or taken a
vacation or, you know, paid their fucking bills without
worrying about it. Money can buy you a lot of happiness. **But you have to stop and ask yourself whether**

the things you've bought and surrounded yourself with are actually making you happy.

Close your eyes and think about how you want your home to feel. Joyful? Calm? Sophisticated? (At no point did you think "chaotic" or "anxiety inducing," right? Didn't think so.) Now imagine what your home would need to look like to create that feeling. **Hold onto that mental image of your ideal space while you're decluttering, and think really hard about keeping anything that isn't In it.** Once you've pared down, you can use a little of that happiness-buying-money to invest in a few things that suit your new style. Let me say that again: a *few* things.

This exercise is super helpful if you're death cleaning for a move. With a little creativity, you can have your individual-size cheesecake and eat it too. You'd be amazed at how many plants an apartment balcony can hold (think lattice and hanging baskets). And bringing blooms inside is proven to increase a person's sense of well-being. Channel your inner millennial and bring home some greenery. Even if your heirs have black thumbs, they'll be happier to inherit a few plants than your entire Cat's Meow collection.

The point is, you don't need to surround yourself with stuff to be happy. You could have a three-story mansion with room for the contents of an entire fucking Target and still be miserable. **Creating your happy place requires being more selective with your stuff.** In other words—you guessed it—decluttering. And by the time you hit happy, you'll probably have nixed a lot of the crap you'd have passed down to unsuspecting successors.

A LITTLE PREP GOES A LONG WAY

Before you declutter so much as a key fob, you need to know what your options are. **Figuring out what you can find a new home for and what you cannot will help you save time and avoid disappointment as you sort through your stuff.** You may as well get used to the idea now: not everything can be rehomed or upcycled.* But finding a new home for as much of your stuff as possible helps you, helps others, and helps the planet. That's a win-win-win, and it's worth a little bit of legwork.

Set aside an hour to make a list of local charities and thrift shops, and find out what types of donations each one takes. (One fucking hour isn't going to kill you. But something else definitely will, so stop whining and get to work.) Some want your furniture, while others don't have the space or the sales volume. An animal shelter might take old bed pillows, but most thrift stores won't touch them with a double-gloved hand.

With so many recalls on kids' stuff, you'll be hard pressed to find an organization willing to take a car seat or a stroller, but you might know a friend or local family in need. Just double-check that recall list before you hand someone a cartoon-dinosaur-adorned death

---

*No one wants your VCR. Literally no one. You might be able to find a recycling center that takes electronics, though. Take responsibility for your purchases—yes, even the ones from the nineties—and look for sustainable solutions before letting anything hit the trash.

trap. And did you know car seats expire? If the expiration date has passed on yours, it goes in the trash.

Once you have an idea of who takes what, jot down a quick list of things you could take to each place on your list. Don't overthink it—you're just training your brain to make the association. A few items have probably popped into your head by now. Those old silver dollars can go to the "We Buy Gold" place up the street. The extra towels could go to the Humane Society. That hutch you never actually liked but kept because it was your husband's mom's can go to the Habitat ReStore while he's fishing with his buddies. You get the idea. (That was a joke, in case you're not sure. Obviously, I don't condone donating things without the owner's express consent, even if it would take your husband the better part of a year to notice.)

As you're sorting through your stuff down the line, your brain should automatically make the connection to a potential drop-off location. That doesn't mean you're automatically going to get rid of the thing. But you'll at least be able to make an informed decision.

And knowing that the local women's shelter could use your kids' old board games might make the decision to donate them a whole lot easier.

Just remember that which places can take what is going to depend a lot on what they have the room and resources for *at that moment*. Always call on the day you plan to make your donation and double-check that the organization can take it. We're not palming shit off on people who don't want it anymore, remember? That's the whole fucking point of this.

YOUR TIME IS WORTH MORE THAN YOUR CABBAGE PATCH KID

Donating your stuff to people who need or want it more than you do is awesome and highly encouraged. But you're not a monster for wanting to recoup some of your costs. After all, if you do this death-cleaning thing right, you're probably watching hundreds of dollars' worth of your stuff walk out the door. And some of it's good stuff. **So why not sell it? Because it's an annoying time suck, that's why not.** And it probably isn't worth as much as you think it is.

That said, there's definitely a little money to be made if you have some time and the patience of a golden retriever with a treat on his nose. **You just need to do some digging to figure out whether your stuff is actually worth selling.** A quick Google search is step one. If you see similar items for sale or articles about them making a comeback, move on to step two: find out what's actually selling. You can search eBay listings by "sold" to see how much items are *really* selling for versus what overly optimistic sellers are *trying* to sell them for. And eBay isn't the only game in town anymore. From clothing marketplaces to local Facebook groups, you can find tailor-made resellers for pretty much everything you own.

If you're still rocking Windows Vista and have no earthly idea how to navigate the world of online resellers, outsource it. You probably have a teen in your life who's open to some light bribery (baked goods, gift cards . . . depends on the teen). Promising them a cut of the profits is even better—it'll light a fire under their ass to get top dollar. ("Top dollar" being relative when you're talking about an old Vera Bradley tote or an American Flyer coal car.)

Thankfully, not all sales require you to bribe children or meet up with complete strangers in the grocery store parking lot.* You can sell most fine jewelry and coins to stores that specialize in them, and vintage or designer clothing can go to thrift shops on commission. Just make sure you ask around or read reviews before choosing your buyer. Some of these places are just one step above used-car dealerships.

Maybe you'll have enough cash to treat yourself to a massage when you're finished decluttering. Or maybe you'll remember that charitable organizations are doing you a huge favor by taking all of your unwanted shit with zero hassle. Whatever gets it out of the house, man.

---

*If you sell stuff online, **never** give out your home address or agree to go to the buyer's house. Always meet somewhere very public during a busy time of day. This isn't a sitcom from the 1950s. It's an after-school special from the 1990s. Stranger danger.

BE SMART ABOUT WHO YOU CHOOSE TO ASK FOR HELP

Friends and loved ones can be a huge help when decluttering. But they can also be a giant pain in the ass. **Think very carefully about who you're talking to before you even bring up the notion of decluttering.** If your niece is the type to drag you down memory lane and make you feel guilty for getting rid of your kid's shitty preschool artwork, you're better off leaving her in the dark about your death-cleaning efforts. If she's ready to break out the bubbly and get to work like Samantha when sorting through Carrie's over-priced walk-in, read her in on day one.

Cheerleaders and straight-talkers are a yes. Sentimental saps and people with their own hoarding tendencies are a no. It's up to you to figure out which is which. If you're having trouble, float a test balloon. Tell your loved ones you're thinking about getting rid of your [insert family heirloom here]. Doesn't matter what it is as long as it's likely to stir up some opinions. **What you're looking for is someone who doesn't talk you into or out of it but instead helps you decide what's best for you. That's your death-cleaning bestie.** Everyone else can sit this ride out until you actually need their input. Which may be never, by the way. This is your shit—you get the final say.

BECOME A DECISION—MAKING MACHINE

Some lucky people get less sentimental as the years pass. That's great for them, and it's good for you if you find yourself able to nonchalantly toss treasured possessions later in life. But you can't count on being one of those people, so you're going to have to suck it up and make some decisions now.

With most things in life, you want to start with the hard stuff and get it out of the way. That is the exact fucking opposite of what you need to do when death cleaning. **You need to build up your "fuck it" muscles and get some momentum going before you tackle anything that's the least bit important to you.** Old photos, family heirlooms, gifts from people you love—all that shit can wait.

Baby steps, baby. First, give yourself an easy win. Clean out a drawer. Just one drawer. It doesn't have to be perfect—it just has to be orderly. Tossing what you don't need, finding homes for the stragglers, and seeing the resulting neatness will have you craving this decluttering high.

Do that a few more times. Recycle the takeout menus (you have Google—what the hell do you need a paper menu for?), throw out all the expired canned goods at the back of the cabinet, sort that stack of papers that's half junk mail you couldn't be bothered to toss. Whatever you choose to do, keep it small.

When you're ready to take things up a notch, start with the stuff that's been pissing you off. Maybe it's the overburdened spice rack that seems to implode every time you reach for the red pepper flakes. Or the work clothes you haven't touched since you retired and discovered leggings. Whatever it is that's driving you crazy, deal with it. You'll feel like you've gone to therapy when you're finished.

The point is to just get started—with anything, at any time, for however long you can. **If you get stuck on something, don't hem and haw. Just move on to something else until your "fuck it" muscles have reached Hemsworth levels.** Thankfully, decluttering gets easier the more you do it. So when you throw a shirt in the "maybe" pile after an hour of mental anguish on day one, rest assured that you'll eventually get that shit down to a brisk two minutes.

DRAW A LINE IN THE SAND AND STICK TO IT

One way to make saying "fuck it" a whole lot easier is by setting a standard for the keepers. Draw a hard line—any object that doesn't meet this criteria goes.

And because it's your line, you can't argue with it. (Well, you can, but your friends may stage an intervention if they see you arguing with yourself over a "live, laugh, love" sign.)

Everyone's criteria are different, but I like to start with the stuff that makes me happy beyond what is typically reasonable for a tee shirt or a stapler.* I don't care if it's a unicorn lawn inflatable that annoys the neighbors. If it brings a smile to my face when I see it or use it, it's a keeper.

That's a purposely lofty metric, though, meant to help you create your happy place. **When you're death cleaning, you're trying to create an intentional space. Happy, yes. But also purposeful. Your criteria need to be a little more rigorous.** A few to consider:

> **Have you used the item in the last six months? (This is a yes-or-no question, and the nos get tossed.)**

---

*My tiny teal stapler makes me happy. Do I use it often? No. Does it make me smile every time I see it? Yes. Will anyone have an existential crisis over it when I'm gone? No. Keeper.

Will you use it in the next six months? (If you think "maybe" is an acceptable answer, you haven't been paying attention. Maybes get tossed.)

Are you keeping it to make someone else happy? (Sweet, but no.)

Are you saving it for someone? (They get it now, or they don't get it at all. And no guilting them into it.)

I saved the best for last: Would I keep this if I were moving and couldn't hire help? When you can afford to hire packers and movers, moving becomes less of an incentive to get your shit together. But when you have to haul that stuff around yourself? You'd be amazed at how much shit you're suddenly ready to let go of. Trust me: you'd rather exercise your "fuck it" muscles than your actual muscles.

USE IT OR LOSE IT APPLIES TO MORE THAN HIGH-SCHOOL FRENCH

If you like your criteria to have a little more kick, this one's for you: use it or lose it. You've got to have pretty big "fuck it" muscles for this one, but it applies to every object in your house, skips right over emotional attachment, and makes quick work of decluttering decisions. It also works a treat on stagnant hobbies.

We prioritize what's important to us. Put another way: if you wanted to, you would have. If you haven't learned how to crochet by now, it's probably safe to ditch that bag of tangled yarn and abandoned scarves. Same goes for the swanky running shoes, soapmaking kit, gardening tools, colorful dumbbell set, and fancy pressure cooker. Trying new things is great. But if you sink money into something and still can't be bothered to give it a go, it's probably not going to happen. **Let go of old dreams (or half-assed hobbies) and make room for new ones.** Because, again, you're not dead yet. There will be new hobbies to half-ass.

TAKE A BREATH— BURNOUT IS A BITCH

Momentum is great, but you also need to pace yourself. There will come a time in the process when you feel "fuck it" deep in your soul and are ready to put everything you own out on the curb. That's not the kind of "fuck it" we're going for here. That's the exhaustion talking. That means you need a break.

Whether you need a day, a week, or an hour-long hot-stone massage, do what you need to do to get back in a productive headspace. Sleeping on a mattress on the floor in the middle of a stark room isn't half as appealing as it sounds when you're in the middle of a nervous breakdown. (Unless you're taking decorating tips from the typical twenty-something guy.)

WORK BACKWARD FROM THE STUFF YOU CAN'T LIVE WITHOUT

You started off taking baby steps, but at some point, you will have to face the inevitable: the larger, more guilt-inducing items you've been avoiding. Thankfully, there's a helpful little exercise you can use to work through these. Imagine you win a remote island villa (the grown-up version of being stranded on a desert island) and can only take your favorite things.

What just popped into your head? Because something definitely did. Make a quick list of things like that—the things that you can't live without. Do **not** spend more than three minutes on your list. The more you think about it, the more shit you'll add to the list. **This is about learning to listen to your gut.**

Knowing what you can't live without throws into stark contrast what you absolutely can live without. Suddenly Grandma's dishes and all those historical biographies you keep saying you're going to read don't make the cut. That's because you're not keeping those things around for you. Maybe you're hanging onto Grandma's dishes out of obligation. And you're lining your bookshelves with crap you don't want to read to impress people whose opinions don't matter. (They really don't, so you can ditch the Tolstoy.)

Your home is your happy place. It should be filled with things that light you up. Guilt, pride, and shame are not those things. Get rid of the fuckers alongside the air mattress.

What are the things you're keeping just for you? What are the things you're keeping with someone else in mind? The latter could be gifts you're not crazy about, heirlooms you couldn't say no to, or heirlooms you're counting on your kids not to say no to. (Clutter is an exasperating and guilt-filled cycle.) **I promise you that your kids will be far more interested in the things that made you happy than in the things you felt obligated to keep.**

PRACTICE MAKES PERFECTLY ADEQUATE DECLUTTERING SKILLS

You don't have to become Marie Kondo overnight to get your shit together. Remember, you are not expected to declutter your entire home in a day. Hell, you don't even have to declutter an entire drawer in a day. (A junk drawer is easily a two-day project.) **You just have to keep at it.**

Keep looking critically at your space and the things in it. Ask yourself what's working for you and what's not. Do little bits of decluttering wherever and whenever you can. (Maybe start with the unopened air fryer sitting in that bottom corner cabinet where kitchen gadgets go to die.) The process will get infinitely easier as you build up those "fuck it" muscles. But here's the secret that professional organizers won't tell you: you don't even have to do this decluttering thing well.

You don't need to have one of those closets that looks like a high-end store selling $500 purses, or a kitchen drawer full of perfectly organized sandwich baggies in little wooden holders. Your bookshelves don't need to be styled like a spread out of a Pottery Barn catalog, with greenery and decor and books infuriatingly placed pages-out. They just need to hold your fucking books. (Although, preferably, far fewer books. Those things are a bitch to box up and move.) Just keep chipping away at the clutter and chaos and, little by little, you'll transform your home.*

MEMORY LANE IS A DEAD—END STREET

When you're just getting started and still building that momentum, you want to avoid sentimental landmines. Those fuckers can blow up all your decluttering progress. Not only are nostalgic items a time suck, they also destroy all your decision-making mojo. Next thing you

---

*Choosing an end date doesn't hurt, though. You don't want to be doing this shit every day for the rest of your life.

know, four hours have gone by, and all you've accomplished is giving yourself secondhand embarrassment by flipping through photos and journals from your angsty teenage years.*

If you come across something that tugs on your heartstrings, set it aside until you've decluttered, well, pretty much everything else. Once you're appropriately numbed to bullshit and schmaltz, then you can tackle the keepsakes. Set aside at least a week for this part, decluttering in short bursts if you need to. Mementos can bring up a lot of emotions, not all of them happy. It's OK to take breaks or circle back to things you're not ready to deal with.

The goal here is to distill all the relics of years gone by down from an attic's worth of crap into a neat little time capsule of favorites. Keep only those things that fill you up with pride, joy, or awe. And keep them handy. **Stuff that stirs up good memories is**

---

*I don't know about you, but if I find a long-forgotten journal from my younger days, I'm just burning the damn thing. No trash, no shredder . . . flames. I don't even need to open it. My most awkward moments are already on a loop in my head. I don't need to see them remastered in 4K.

only worth the space it's taking up if you're able to actively enjoy it. Your daughter's old wooden rocking horse, on the other hand, could be bringing joy to another little one right now instead of doing its best impression of a sparkly gargoyle.

Photos are some of the worst offenders here. At least in the old days, when you had to pay for film, you were a lot less likely to take hundreds of pictures of your sleeping cat. (Guilty.) So the photos you have to sort through probably hold some pretty great memories and frameable moments. But what fucking good are they doing stuffed in plastic storage bins? Time to dig them out and make some sense of that mess.

Not sure who those people are staring back at you? Yeah, you probably should have labeled those. If you're lucky enough to have friends and family with good memories, put them to work. In fact, make it a party. Some snacks, cold drinks, and good company armed with pens and ready to reminisce? Sounds like a hell of a night. And at the end of it, you can send everyone home with their own little time capsules. Win-win.

LOOK INTO EACH OBJECT'S FUTURE

We talked about taking the long view when it comes to death cleaning. That means asking yourself what happens to your stuff when you're gone. **While you're assessing each object for its happy-place potential, channel your inner fortune teller and try to see its future.** Come on, you know you've always thought you were a little bit psychic. Put that intuition to the test!

Will that autographed baseball make someone else happy? Will it make someone unhappy? Will it cause a fight? (You would be amazed at the shit family members will fight over.) Once you have your answers, you can make an informed decision about what to do with it. Maybe you gift the ball to the family sports fan while you're alive to see the joy it brings them. And to avoid leaving it to your son, who's still traumatized from his T-ball tryouts. Maybe you sell the fucker to avoid family drama. Or maybe you let your family know that they can get rid of it guilt-free when you're gone. Whatever the future holds, make a plan for it.

If you're not sure where people stand on things, just ask. Ask friends and family what they want *and* what they don't want long before you need to make any decisions. If they say "yes," you don't have to give it to them now, but it might make you both happier in the long run if you do. If they say "no," don't argue. In fact, let people know up front that they're not going to hurt your feelings if they don't want your shit. (We've talked about this. It's literally the title of the book. If it's going to hurt your feelings, either get a thicker skin or don't offer the thing up in the first place.) Nobody needs more pressure in their life. Smile and suck it up.

You can't stop time by clinging to all your crap. But you can make life easier and happier for yourself and for the people you love by putting even the tiniest fucking bit of thought into what happens to all of it. Not a bad trade-off.

REMEMBER WHAT THEY SAY ABOUT ASSUMING

So, you're looking forward to the day you can pass down your collection of Revolutionary War miniatures to your kids. Do they know that? Do they seem excited by the prospect? Or do they avoid eye contact?

Never assume that someone is cool with being on the receiving end of your death-cleaning spree. The whole "one day, all of this will be yours" thing only works if you're handing down an actual kingdom, not a cardboard battlefield full of tiny minutemen. For things like that, you've got to communicate your intentions.

Any healthy relationship requires good communication. But communication is a two-way radio, not a podcast. **Talk to your loved ones about your hopes for all your stuff, then take your finger off the fucking button and listen when they tell you how they feel about it.** (Timing is everything, though. See "Be smart about who you choose to ask for help" on page 68.)

If you want to take the pressure off, tell your family members that you were thinking of donating your collection but wanted to see if any of them were interested first. If, however, passing down those tiny soldiers is really important to you, then let it be known. Life's too fucking short not to be real with the people you love. Plus, your kids might see that set in a new light if they know it means that much to you.*

That kind of consideration applies to secondhand gifts of all sizes and kinds, not just the important stuff. And it's crucial when giving stuff to kids who aren't yours (yes, even if they're related to you). You want people to think of you fondly when you're gone, not curse your name for giving their death-metal-obsessed daughter a drum kit. Unless you want to be the focus of a hastily made voodoo doll, always get the parents' express permission before giving their kid so much as a stick of gum.

---

*If their mouth says "sure" but their eyes signal that they're in some sort of hostage situation, consider finding another home for those miniatures anyway.

REHOME THE LAUNDRY CHAIR

One outside-the-box way to cut back on the clutter? **Get rid of the things that attract clutter.** That chair that sits in the corner of your bedroom, collecting clothes in various degrees of cleanliness? Ditch it. No chair, no place to put your not-quite-dirty jeans.

Obviously, for this to work, you have to have some kind of line you're not willing to cross. If you'll just pile your shit on the floor where the chair was, this technique probably isn't for you. But maybe seeing that pile will shame you into throwing those clothes in a drawer or a hamper. (Probably the first time you slip on yesterday's jeans and there's a six-legged stowaway in tow. You'll never forget the feeling of that little fucker crawling up your leg.)

OR USE THE LAUNDRY CHAIR TO YOUR ADVANTAGE

Another option is to take a closer look at the things that attract clutter. That chair is where all the stuff you're actually using ends up. Which items never make it to the chair? Which ones are perpetually left in the drawers when it's time to do laundry? If you're not using it, stop letting it take up space in your home.

The same goes for shoes that end up by the door, pens on the desk, makeup in the bathroom, and so much more. **Look at the stuff that stays put instead of worrying about the crap that you're actively using.** That untouched stuff can probably go. And once it does, you'll have more space and a better idea of how to effectively organize the shit you use regularly.

CLOTHING
Childlike optimism is for children, loving yourself is for adults

Time for some tough love. (Or, *more* tough love.) You're never going to fit into those skinny jeans again because life is too short to give up cake and toaster pastries. That's not a bad thing. If death cleaning makes you realize anything, it's just how fucking short life is. Shouldn't it also be sweet? (Yes. The answer is yes. You deserve toaster pastries.)

Maybe you're twenty pounds heavier than you'd really like to be. Or maybe your body doesn't conform to whatever crazy standards they're airbrushing people into these days. But think of all your body has been through in your life—all the stress, strain, excitement, and joy. From climbing the rope in gym glass to creating life, our bodies do a lot for us. And we reward them with annoyance, scorn, and guilt.

We're done with that bullshit. **Accept where you are in life. Appreciate your body for putting up with your**

shit.* Wear clothes that celebrate it, and ditch the stuff that doesn't. Opening your dresser drawers every day and seeing jeans that make you feel bad about yourself is not a worthwhile use of your energy or space.

Be just as realistic about what you need as what you don't

You've got dreams of a minimalist closet with thirty-two pieces of clothing that you can mix and match for all occasions. But we can't all be Zuckerberg. If you're a person in the real world, you need different shit for different occasions and seasons. And you're lucky if three things in your closet are multipurpose.

If you can find some go-to pieces that can be dressed up and down for all occasions, great. But more likely, you're going to need more than a few items on hand so you're ready for any occasion. There's nothing wrong with that. **No one wants to be scrambling to find a funeral dress at the last minute.**

_____

*Sit up straight and do some neck rolls right now. There is no piece of clothing that will hide severe text-neck.

Sure, decision fatigue is a real thing. But who wants to wear all black every day? Or all tee shirts? You're allowed to express all facets of your personality with your wardrobe. In fact, I encourage it. Life would be boring if everyone went the Zuckerberg route of wearing the same fucking tee shirt and jeans every day. But you've collected a random smattering of things based on your taste at the time, what stores were selling, whether you've had a shitty day, and who you were dating. That calls for some decluttering. **See if you can tailor your closet to your current needs and keep shit to a minimum.**

You have lived too long to own shitty clothing

No one wants to think about the fact that they could get hit by a bus tomorrow. But do you really want to risk the EMTs cutting away your clothes to find the rattiest pair of underwear you own? That embarrassment will follow you into the afterlife.

You are a grown-ass adult. It's time to ditch the shit that's seen better days and admit you're never going to darn your fucking socks. But we're not throwing clothes in the trash anymore. And we're not taking ratty crap to thrift stores. We're taking responsibility for our clutter.

According to the EPA, more than 80 percent of clothing ends up in landfills. That includes a lot of the stuff that people pawn off on thrift stores knowing damn well it's not fit to resell. Luckily, clothing recyclers are a thing. If you can't find a local organization, retailers like H&M and For Days will recycle your old clothes. That clothing gets broken down and upcycled into new pieces.

So, gather up all your clean worn-out underwear, holey socks, pilly sweaters, and anything else you'd be mortified for a hot EMT to see you in, and recycle it now. Then invest in fewer, better quality pieces going forward. (This is all for nothing if you don't learn your fucking lesson.)

Ask yourself what it's worth to you

You don't have to pack your closet like you're playing a game of Tetris made for hoarders. It's OK to leave a little breathing room around your clothes. And if you've got nice, brand-name clothing, that should be the goal. You've invested in good pieces—now give them room to shine. And to avoid snags.

Feeling a little hesitant to give up those finer pieces? **If you've got the goods, online resellers are a great place to get a little extra cash for quality clothing.** Unlike listing a dresser in a Facebook group or on Craigslist, selling clothing on sites like Poshmark and The RealReal is relatively painless.* You make some money, your clothing goes to a good home, and your closet can breathe.

---

*Try to avoid the urge to shop while you're browsing for the sake of price comparison. I'm not saying never—just while you're decluttering. Once you know what you need, these sites are a great way to get it without spending a fortune or contributing to the fast-fashion problem.

DECOR
You shouldn't need a storage unit for seasonal decor

If you're the type of person who goes all out for every season and holiday, with interior touches and exterior displays, then I applaud you. You're a far less lazy person than I am. But how many seasonal decorations do you fucking need?

I say this with love because my mom is one of those people. She has an incredible knack for making everything beautiful and homey, adding seasonal touches to every room until the house looks like something out of a Hallmark movie. The woman could have her own HGTV show. And it's something she loves to do.

It also takes time, energy, and a shit-ton of space. I'm talking bins and bins *and bins* of seasonal decorations. Florals, wall hangings, garlands, lights, candles, vases, those colorful little pebbles people put in vases—you name it, she's got it. And she's got it all in a storage unit. (Do you remember Joanna Gaines's barn full of decor and furniture from the early days of the show? If my mom could, she would.)

It's a lot. And, as a deeply lazy person, I'm not wild about the idea of inheriting a storage unit's worth of decorations. So we've reached a compromise. Every season, she goes through the bins and immediately separates out anything she's not loving anymore. And every season, she ends up taking a bin or two to the thrift store. Progress over perfection, remember?

The goal for seasonal decor is the same as the goal for everything else: to have a curated collection of the things you love. I'm sure my mom's collection will fit inside the house eventually. (Pretty sure, anyway.) And I'll be happy to inherit the things she loved most and make my home just as warm and inviting as she did. Or at least warmer and more inviting than it was. (*Deeply* lazy.)

Recognize when you don't even see it anymore

You wouldn't believe the amount of stuff sitting in your home right now that, if hobgoblins stole it in the night, you wouldn't even notice was gone. And I'm not just talking about the shit that's been sitting in boxes in the garage, keeping the mice comfy for the past ten years. I'm talking about the shit you were so excited to buy and bring home and hang on your walls.

It's not entirely your fault. **Our brains can only hold so much information. They need to prioritize, and a painting that's been on your wall for a year doesn't top the list.** It's the same reason the Post-it Notes all over your office have ceased to be helpful reminders.

Sure, you can move shit around to keep it fresh and force your brain to take notice. But when you do, take a minute to ask yourself whether it's worth it. Considering you didn't remember that painting existed five minutes ago, maybe you don't need it.

Be real. When's the last time you noticed those garden gnomes you've been desperately collecting for years? Do you delight in finding them, then promptly forget they exist? Once they've served their purpose, why not allow someone else to enjoy them? (That someone will find them at your local thrift shop. Do not foist them on some unsuspecting family member.) Focus on keeping the shit that's worth noticing.

STORAGE AREAS
If you can't fit a car in your garage, you have missed the point

Attics, basements, garages, and storage units are prime locations for lazy clutter—the kind you allow to take up space because it's not in your direct eyeline, nagging you. Just because you have the space to store something doesn't mean you should. If it's in a box and it's not holiday decorations, you probably haven't laid eyes on it in years. **"Out of sight, out of mind" is not an effective mantra for death cleaning.** Someone's going to have to deal with that shit eventually, so it damn well better be you now.

Decluttering means taking stock of every object in your house and deciding whether it's earning its keep. That includes lazy clutter. What good is a garage that's so full of crap that it can't house your car? (Have you seen the size of hail these days?) What good is that LEGO set that's sitting in a box in your basement? Remember, we're letting go of whatever doesn't fit the life we have now. Intentions don't count. Actions do.

If you dream of a dedicated LEGO space with elaborate displays, get on it. Clear out the rest of that basement and turn it into your own little wonderland of colored blocks and mini-figurines. But if that shit's going to spend the next decade in a box, it would be better off going to someone who's thrilled to be elbow-deep in LEGOs every day.

Whether you use your lazy clutter or lose it, take back control of your home and the stuff that's taking up space in it. Attics and basements are for ghosts and pool tables, not seventh-grade participation trophies. Declutter accordingly.

Storage units are an expensive cry for help

Storage units are the new drugstores—they're on every corner. But I'm willing to bet yours is more than a few miles away from your house. That means you're only going there sporadically, if at all. More likely, that's where you keep all the stuff you don't need or use but don't know what else to do with. So why are you paying someone your hard-earned money to store shit you don't even want?

This is how much we, as human beings, don't want to deal with our shit. We are willing to throw away thousands of dollars to store things we don't actually give a damn about. That's a weeklong vacation, right there. In Fiji.

Storage units should never be a permanent solution. Instead, they should be a way station on your decluttering journey. The extra space can help you get some things out of the way while you focus on others, especially if you've just inherited the results of someone else's lack of death cleaning.* It can also help you see the potential in your space (you know, by letting you remove all the crap that's getting in its way).

Once you've gotten what you need out of a storage unit, it's time to get your life and your money back. If you're an empty nester who's downsized from a house to an apartment, then you need to downsize your stuff too. Odds are pretty fucking good you're not going to want to upsize later. If the remnants of your bachelor pad are in storage and you're now a happy dad of three, let that eyesore of a black leather couch go. The stuff you own should support the life you have now, not haunt you from an overpriced garage like the Ghost of Hangovers Past.

---

*Temporarily storing someone's stuff after they've passed until you have time to deal with it is fine. Letting it sit there, undealt with, for months and years on end? Not fine. Sorry to say, that mess is now your problem. Deal with it, and let it be a lesson to you.

RANDOM CRAP
If it doesn't have a home, its home is in the trash

I'm bringing this one back from *Tidy the F*ck Up* because it's worth repeating. And because social media has turned me on to a fun new phrase: doom boxes. This trendy name for the Island of Misfit Crap refers to the (hopefully) little bins of miscellaneous items that don't have homes. But if your kitchen cabinet or hall closet fits the description, they too can be doom boxes. It's a delightfully inclusive expression.

Doom boxes are some of the most befuddling bits of clutter because they're often the result of decluttering. They contain the leftover bits and bobs that defy organization, plus the crap you just didn't feel like dealing with. But the time has come to face your clutter demons.

Start by putting away anything that actually does have a home and ended up in the box out of sheer laziness. Then throw out anything that doesn't work, needs mending, or belongs to something you no longer own. You'd be amazed at how much junk you can clear out with just those two steps. (Don't get too excited. We're not done yet.)

Finally, put whatever's left to the test: Do you use it, love it, or plan to gift it to someone? That last one's pretty unlikely, considering these boxes tend to be full of old charger cables, loose buttons, and broken pens. If it's a yes, the item gets its own place of honor in your home. Which is to say, somewhere you will actually remember it exists and use it (or gift it). If it's a no—and most things will be—it immediately goes in the garbage or the donate box.*

When you're all done decluttering the recently decluttered, you can donate your doom box in triumph. You know, so you're not immediately tempted to start adding to it again. (If nothing else, we are creatures of fucking habit.)

---

*While I understand wanting to wait until you have a lot to donate before heading to the thrift store, a donate box should never sit around for more than a week. That way, you won't be tempted to take things out of it, and the thrift-store employees won't be tempted to punch you in the face for donating ten fucking tubs of stuff at once.

There are no forgotten million-dollar antiques in your attic

Hopefully, the possibility of uncovering hidden riches isn't your only motivation for decluttering. The idea that you're going to dust off an old plate or painting you find in your attic and discover a long-lost treasure worth millions is a lot like the idea that you're going to hit Powerball. Could it happen? Absolutely. Will it happen? Probably not. And by probably not, I mean you have a better chance of being eaten by a shark. In Idaho.

Holding onto shit because you think it might be worth something someday is crazy. Have we learned nothing from Beanie Babies? Google is free. If you can't figure out an object's value online, you can at least find a human who will figure it out for you. Go get that shit appraised before hanging all your hopes and caviar dreams on it. Then you can drop it off at the thrift store on your way home from finding out it's not worth a damn thing. (Hey, you can always sell that old Bowflex in the basement. That's got to be worth at least a hundred bucks.)

Although long-lost Monets are a long shot, you may find some real treasures buried in the box-filled corners of your home. **Photos, family heirlooms, and memories that you can share with loved ones may not buy you a retirement villa in Tuscany, but they are arguably more valuable than anything that would pique the interest of *Pawn Stars*.** And so is all the fucking space they're taking up. That attic could be a home office if you clean it up.

You shouldn't be able to supply an Office Depot from your home office

The older you are, the more likely you are to have a treasure trove of office supplies in the form of printer cables, disks, and mouse pads you haven't needed since the dawn of the twenty-first century. Not to mention dozens of branded pens. Time to cull the herd.

The nineties are over. We're not doing fax machines and CD-ROMs anymore. If you have any floppy disks lying around—seriously, you still own floppy disks??—throw them out now. You don't own anything that can read them anyway. I know you want to think of them as tiny time capsules, but they're probably full of essays and AIM conversations from junior high. Save yourself the brain cells and toss them.*

In the age of digital . . . everything . . . you probably need a laptop, its charger, and *maybe* a mouse (if it's optical—and it should be—no mouse pad needed). On the off chance you need to print something, you can go to an actual office-supply store. It'll save you from spending sixty bucks every time the fucking ink in your printer dries out from lack of use.

That cold medicine stopped working five years ago

No, you don't have to throw out everything in your medicine cabinet that's expired. Expiration dates on over-the-counter meds are more about covering the company's ass than they are about accurately

---

*Break them, then throw them out. You might not have a disk reader anymore, but you never know who does and would love to go through your old AIM conversations. Never underestimate the creepy weirdness of other people.

predicting when a medication's past its prime. According to experts, that bottle of ibuprofen is good for a few years after its expiration date. But some meds, especially those in liquid form, lose their effectiveness more quickly.

When you're barking like a dog whose owner fell down a well, do you really want to take half-assed cough syrup? No. You want the good shit. So take a few minutes every six months or so to update your medicine cabinet.

What you really need to worry about are the prescription meds. These aren't meds you keep "just in case." If you need more, you ask your doctor or pharmacist. But if you leave them lying around, they could fall into the wrong hands. Make a habit of dropping off unused prescriptions at your local pharmacy for disposal as soon as you know you're finished with them. Do **not** flush pharmaceuticals of any kind down the toilet—they can pollute lakes and streams and even end up in our drinking water. We're decluttering *mindfully*, remember?

Buying a cookbook and making a recipe are not the same thing

With an entire internet's worth of delicious recipes for every occasion and taste, it's hard to argue for keeping any cookbooks. But this process isn't about getting rid of stuff you love. So if you love using your cookbooks—hell, even if you just love looking at them—keep them. But, if you bought those cookbooks in a flurry of hunger and good intentions and now find your interest waning, out they go!

You can always snap pics of your favorite recipes and keep them in a folder on your tablet, saving yourself the shelf space and mental energy that those cookbooks occupied. (Plus, you can zoom in on that tiny type.) More often than not, those are going to be the recipes that are worth clinging to. **Recipes passed down from family members, gifted by thoughtful friends, kept from your favorite meals—those are the ones worth keeping.** (Those get decluttered too, though. Obviously.)

If you really need the feel of a cookbook, organize your favorites into a binder filled with plastic sheets so they're easier to find and harder to ruin when the pasta sauce inevitably splatters. And if it's just the obnoxiously saccharine life stories at the top of every fucking online recipe that are keeping you from enjoying all the internet has to offer, I've got you covered. Save yourself some aggravation by looking for the little "jump to recipe" button at the top of the page. Mary Jean of "Live, Laugh, Bake" will never know.

How many fucking screwdrivers do you need?

Being handy is great, especially when you own a home. But handy people tend to collect tools. And supplies. And lumber. Next thing you know, you have to build onto your garage to store it all. (Because that's the sort of thing handy people do.) **News flash: you're not opening a fucking hardware store.** You don't need every tool Ryobi makes or every type of nut, bolt, and screw in existence. Keep what you need for current projects and cull the rest.

When you have leftovers from a project that you know you won't use in the (very) near future, you can find plenty of people and organizations who would be happy to have them. And don't forget that you can return unopened items to the store. Of all the stupid things to waste money on, 3-inch wood screws shouldn't make the list.

DON'T EVEN THINK ABOUT HAVING A YARD SALE

Have you ever tried to sell . . . anything? Even when you sell stuff online, you end up spending weeks weeding through all the lowballs and trade offers until you find a buyer willing to pay anything close to your price. You have to play the long game to get the goods. But more often than not, you compromise just to get the damn thing out the door. Sound like fun? Well, yard sales are worse.

You have to make sure an item is in saleable condition, then organize it, price it, and display it. You also have to register your sale with the town, pay a fee, advertise it, and create visible signage. Plus, you have to stand there all day and haggle with strangers over the value of your stuff. I don't know about you, but I'd rather get a root canal. If you really need a hard deadline to light a fire under your ass (and the looming specter of death isn't doing it for you), try to get in on a neighborhood sale. At least they cut down on some of the legwork.

Unless you have something for the collectors in the crowd (power tools, vintage dishware, luxury bags), your ass is waking up at 6 a.m.* and working all damn day to make pennies on the dollar for each of your beloved items. Price your stuff any higher than that, and it becomes curb candy by closing time—and the yard-salers know it. They live for this shit. They spend their week scanning local papers for sale announcements, work up a weekend schedule, and hit

---

*Yes, you posted that your yard sale begins at 8 a.m. Yes, you even wrote "no early birds" in the announcement. But that's not going to stop some bargain-hunting jackass from knocking on your door at 7 a.m. for a first look. Ask me how I know.

every last one. So don't think they won't wait you out. The good news is that you can put literally anything out on the curb, and it'll be gone by sunup.

WHEN ALL ELSE FAILS, BRING IN THE BIG GUNS

Maybe you're down to your most difficult items or you've been stuck in your head from the start, but a little moral support can make all the difference. Ask your most openly opinionated and supportive friend to come over for particularly tricky decluttering sessions.* No pushovers allowed—enabling your desire to keep the things you know you shouldn't isn't helpful.

Not everyone fits that description, so be selective. You need a ride-or-die bestie for this. If you know someone who can tell you when a dress makes you

---

*Lack of proximity is a lame excuse in the digital age. You can debate the merits of your Flintstone jelly-glass collection just as easily over Zoom as you can in person.

look anemic but gets why you want to hang on to that raggedy tee from the T-Swift concert (and was probably there with you), they're your best bet for breaking through your blocks.

Whether or not you have a friend who can bring the tough love, simply having an accountability partner is a psychological trick worth trying. You could even post your progress to your social media accounts. Nothing lights a fire under your ass like people watching and waiting for you to fail. (If you know someone's actually waiting for you to fail, though, please block that asshole. Unless you're motivated by pettiness. Then shine on, friend.)

REALIZE THAT PERFECTION IS A SHITTY GOAL

Notice that the word "perfect" doesn't appear on the list of benefits on page 4. That's because perfection is bullshit. Those Instagram posts you see of a beautifully appointed kitchen with counters clear of anything but a sage-colored KitchenAid mixer and a eucalyptus branch in a vase? Just out of frame are laundry baskets filled with papers, crayons, utensils, bruised fruit, and everything else that asshole cleared off the counters before hitting the shutter button. And don't even get me started on what's hiding behind those many, many cabinet doors.

Perfection is not attainable. Period. Even trying to be perfect is exhausting and annoying as fuck. So let's stop trying. **Perfect isn't the goal. Happy is.** If you can have designated color-coded cubbies for your kids' shit, great. If all you can manage is a basket by the door, also great. Every little bit helps. Remember, the real question is whether your shit is working for you. Do you use it? Does it make you happy? Do you have a plan for its future? If the answer to all those questions is "yes," then that's your version of perfect. And it's damn sure good enough.

Chapter 3 Checklist

- [ ] Decide you're going to do the damn thing
- [ ] Envision your perfect space, then chip away at whatever doesn't fit into it
- [ ] Figure out which places will take your shit before you start
- [ ] Realize that most things aren't worth the time it would take to sell them
- [ ] Make sure the people you ask for help are actually fucking helpful
- [ ] Build up your "fuck it" muscles by starting small
- [ ] Decide on your criteria for the keepers, then try not to talk yourself out of it
- [ ] Admit that if you haven't used it by now, you probably won't
- [ ] Don't just power through—take breaks when you need them
- [ ] Learn to listen to your gut so you don't have a chance to rationalize bad decisions
- [ ] Focus on progress, not perfection, which is bullshit anyway
- [ ] Don't dig into the sentimental shit until you're a decision-making ninja
- [ ] Take the time to figure out where all your stuff will end up when you're gone

- ☐ Gift the good stuff now, while you're alive to enjoy the effects
- ☐ Never assume someone wants what you want to give them
- ☐ Take a closer look at the places in your home that attract clutter
- ☐ Recycle or sell old clothing instead of letting it end up in the trash
- ☐ Surround yourself with decor you love
- ☐ Stop using storage areas as an excuse to keep shit you don't want
- ☐ Deal with your doom boxes once and for all
- ☐ Stop treating your attic like a fucking museum
- ☐ Act like you live in the digital age and streamline your home office
- ☐ Clean out your medicine cabinet without poisoning any fish
- ☐ Clear out all those complicated recipes you can't be bothered to make
- ☐ Stop storing lumber in your garage so you have room for a fucking car
- ☐ Avoid yard sales at all costs (unless someone else is doing the heavy lifting)
- ☐ Prioritize happiness, not other peoples' opinions

4
Get Your Sh*t Together

GET YOUR AFFAIRS IN ORDER SO YOUR KIDS DON'T HAVE TO

When you die, do you want your kids to reminisce about all the great times you had together? Or do you want them to end up in a blood feud over who gets the Le Creuset? You laugh, but that shit happens all the time. More likely, though, your kids will just curse your name and fight over who gets stuck cleaning out the attic. You already know who it's going to be too. Do you really want your favorite kid resenting you? (Yeah, yeah, you "don't have favorites.")

I'm going to bottom-line this for you one more time: **This is your mess. It's your responsibility to clean it up.** I don't care if your kids are real or hypothetical at this point. Hell, I don't care if your kids have four legs and fur. That just means whoever gets stuck with your crap won't have a sense of obligation forcing them to care what happens to it. You want Cousin Edna rifling through your shit and making decisions about your collector's-edition Arby's drinking glasses? Trick question—she shouldn't have to! (And she'd definitely keep those glasses. Fast-food glassware was oddly chic.)

You chose to bring all of this shit into your house. From the library's worth of bargain books you couldn't live without to the $1,200 exercise bike that you predictably used twice before it became a stupidly expensive towel rack, you have to own your choices. And you want to. **The feelings of freedom and power that come with getting your shit together are pretty damn intoxicating.** You know what else is neat? Not being a burden to your loved ones.

Decluttering is just the beginning. Next up: putting what's left in some sort of recognizable order. And if you're going full death cleaning, that includes your digital life, finances, and final arrangements as well as your video-game collection. Just remember the goal: to take control of your fucking life (and eventual death). Or to ensure that your favorite child doesn't spit on your grave. Whatever works for you.

ASK FOR HELP WHEN YOU NEED IT—JUST NOT FROM YOUR KIDS

We live our whole, messy, complicated lives entwined with a variety of other people. So why anyone would think we could deal with the end of those lives by ourselves, I don't know. You need professional help for appraisals, arrangements, and legal docs. A very good friend who can bring the brutal honesty (and maybe also a very good bottle of wine to help the brutal honesty go down) couldn't hurt either.

The professional help starts with a good lawyer. Sure, you could DIY your will and other documents. But between your stuff, your money, your online accounts, and your final arrangements, there's a lot of shit to deal with. I don't know about you, but I'd rather spend a little cash to make sure I don't end up buried at sea instead of cremated on land. A lawyer can also help you work the system so you don't leave your loved ones hanging. Little things like adding someone as a beneficiary on your bank account can save them months of waiting on the bank to get around to paying them out. And those bills stack up fast when you die!

What you don't need is to burden your loved ones—especially your kids—with all of the decisions you haven't taken the time to work through. They have skin in the game. And unless you've raised obnoxious little assholes, they're probably hesitant to hurt your feelings by telling you how they really feel about your Star Wars collectibles. **Work through your shit, *then* let them know where you could really use their input.** (The extent of that input is going to depend a lot on your relationships with your kids and their general helpfulness. Maybe don't ask the one who loads cups into the dishwasher open-side up.)

HEIRLOOMS
Approach potential inheritors with the same caution as wild animals

If you're the glue that holds your family together, don't be surprised if splitting up your stuff tears them apart. I mean, you won't be here to care about it. But if "uh-oh" just crossed your mind, you might be someone who wants to think about preempting potential hostility.

The drama is real. **If more than one person stands to inherit from you when you're gone, you're going to want to be very careful with this part of the process.** Hopefully, you've raised kind, honest, respectful humans who know how to communicate with each other. But it's hard to know how anyone will handle their grief. Or their jealousy.

You might think nothing of asking Kathleen whether she wants your mother's ring—after all, they were really close. But now her sister is pissed, and you've accidentally ignited a family turf war that will manifest itself in decades of passive aggression. Do you want to spend every holiday playing referee or stuffing your face with pie? Option B, obviously.

Try to get a little intel before you offer or will anyone anything. You could ask someone who has the inside scoop but isn't interested themselves, or you could just ask the girls themselves what items of yours they might want to have someday. Leave it open ended and see if anyone feels strongly. You'll probably be surprised by some of the answers you get.

Once you know where things stand, you can gift sought-after items to friends and family now and share in their joy. **Just make sure you divvy up everything else in writing so that no one has to make tough decisions when you're gone.** If all else fails, you can sell or donate anything that's poised to cause contention without consulting another soul. Lest that cause a pang of guilt, remember this: It's your stuff. You can do whatever the fuck you want with it.

You can't stop people from fighting over stupid shit. And frankly, other people's relationships are not your problem—whether you're alive to hear about them or not. But putting a little thought into the issue now means you can rest easy later, knowing you've done your best to help your family avoid assholery.

Your kid probably doesn't want your wedding dress

That classically elegant dress that's been passed down for generations and miraculously looks just as fabulous on each wearer? You saw that in a movie. That shit doesn't happen in real life.

Too many wedding dresses sit in storage, waiting for the day they can be passed down, only for that day to never come. For one thing, fewer people than ever are tying the knot. For another, wedding dresses are possibly the most personal of fashion decisions. Tastes change, body types differ, and people realize that styles from the eighties should stay in the eighties. Plus, shopping for a wedding dress is the second most fun part of planning a wedding. (I think we can all agree that the first is cake tasting.)

Thrifting is a whole thing these days, so it doesn't hurt to ask whether someone wants your dress. But you have to be prepared to take "no" for an answer. Even if they do take it, they'll probably make alterations to it. That could be anything from resizing it to slicing it up and using it for parts. Are you cool with that?

If you think you're ready to let go, but you'd just rather not see the sausage get made, donating the dress to a thrift store or charity that specializes in occasion dresses is the way to go. You still get to help make someone else's happily ever after happen. And if you don't throw a tantrum over it, your kid might even let you take part in helping them pick out their own wedding dress. (Two words of advice to keep you from getting kicked out of the boutique: *smile* and *breathe*.)

They don't want the antiques either

Imagine giving someone an antique bed set that looks like a prop from *The Haunting* without asking them. Insane, right? Why do we think it's suddenly OK if we bequeath it to them, then? If you want creepy little hand-carved cherubs looking over you while you sleep, that's your business. But gifting that to someone without asking them first is a random act of violence.

You might think Great-Grandma's hutch or the roll-top desk you got at the flea market doesn't fall into the same category as furniture that looks like it might actually be possessed. You would be wrong. For someone who's not into older furniture—a lot of which is dark, heavy, and wooden—all that shit looks the same.

Mid-century modern and light colors are having a moment, probably thanks to a generation who thrived on minimalist IKEA furniture. So maybe antique furniture will have its day. **Either way, remember this: just because you like it doesn't mean they'll like it.** And you won't know unless you talk to them about it. Asking people what they want and listening to their responses will improve your relationships. Foisting ugly-ass antiques on them will not.

The good dishes are probably headed for the rage room

Choosing a china pattern for your "good dishes" used to be a rite of passage. But the number of people who have a separate set of dishes for special occasions is quickly dwindling. Why pay more for dishes you're going to use less? Grab some colorful chargers and napkin rings at Target, and you can set a gorgeous table with your everyday dishes cheaply and on a whim.

If the expense were the only problem, you'd be justified in holding onto Grandma's dishes for the next generation. But it's not. A delicate floral pattern may have been your cup of tea (literally), but your kids could have completely different taste. And why house two complete sets when you can put that space to better use? We've talked about that fucking hutch full of untouched dishes.

Those dishes are also a lot more delicate than the indestructible stuff you can buy today. For one thing, they can't go in the dishwasher, and I don't know who the hell has the time to be handwashing an entire set of dishes after every damn meal. I know I don't. And if you break one, the guilt is swift and severe. Those dishes are irreplaceable.

That's a lot of responsibility for some fucking dishes, so listen when your kid says "no" to taking them. You might be able to find a buyer, depending on the dishes' age and the rarity of the pattern. If you can't, there are worse things than donating them . . . like leaving them to your ungrateful offspring, who will take them to the nearest rage room* and smash the shit out of them. Better to give those dishes at least a chance at finding a new home with someone who appreciates them.

---

*Rage rooms are a great place to donate stuff that would otherwise be headed for the trash. These are places where people pay to smash shit. (Yes, that's really a thing.) They'll take pretty much anything that some-one would pay to hit with a baseball bat.

Costume jewelry is for tea parties and drag shows

When my grandmother passed, my mom inherited a ton of jewelry. Some of it was fine jewelry, like the rings Grandma got for her work anniversaries at the nursing home. (You know, back when companies gave a flying fuck about employee loyalty and handed out gold watches at retirement.) But most of it came from Avon.

If you're not familiar, Avon was one of the earlier multilevel-marketing companies. (The legit, Tupperware kind. Not the scammy, Allez-Vous kind, à la *Schitt's Creek*.) Their jewelry was cheap and cute, and my grandmother bought a ton of it. Although my mom loved that the jewelry reminded her of her mom, it didn't hold the same value—sentimental or real—as the good stuff. And when you can't close your jewelry box anymore, it's going to be the costume jewelry that goes.

If you take the time to look into your jewelry's future, you can pretty much guess whether it's going

to be well loved or tossed in the trash. So be selective about the pieces you choose to pass down. You might think the mood ring you got in a cereal box when you were five is cool (and it totally is), but you know it's headed for the donate bin either way. Take it to the thrift store yourself alongside any other pieces you don't wear or love beyond reason. Your jewelry box shouldn't be one more thing someone else has to declutter.

Once you have a collection of jewelry you love and use, think about the pieces you hope to leave to loved ones. I know I sound like broken record, but gifting the meaningful stuff while you're alive is a hell of a lot more fun for everyone involved than willing shit away. Give it a try. I think you'll agree.*

---

*If it's not enjoyable, it's probably because you didn't put enough thought into the exchange. The point is to gift things that people actually want. If you don't do your due diligence, any eye rolls or gritted teeth are on you.

DOCUMENTS
Clean out your damn computer

If you haven't decluttered your digital spaces, it's time. Your computer is probably the messiest thing in your house. But you have folders, you say. Is everything neatly tucked away and labeled in those folders? Or do you have a full download queue and a bunch of screen-grabs with twenty-six-letter file names? Thought so.

You might look at your computer and see organized chaos, but someone else will look at it and see one of those murder boards with red string running from thumbtack to thumbtack. You know how to find what you're looking for. If someone else needs to find something, they're fucked.

Now, that could be a "them" problem. After all, it's your computer. You're the one who needs to use it every day and know where the hell everything is. But if you get hit by a bus tomorrow, will you be cool with someone digging around in there to get what they need? (Keep in mind, you might not be dead. You might just be in the hospital and need a neighbor to access your insurance info.)

If that fills you with dread, work toward a happy medium. **Spend a few minutes a week going through your files while you watch TV**. Anything that's objectively important gets labeled and organized into easy-to-find folders. Anything that's not gets tossed into the junk folder of your choosing. Don't forget to sort your screengrabs and downloads accordingly. And for fuck's sake, empty your trash.

Learn the difference between important and unimportant

No, you do not fucking need to keep your cable bills for the last twelve months. In fact, there's precious little you can't find with a quick login to your accounts. And if you can find them online in under a minute, they damn well better not be in a filing cabinet in your home.

We're not doing paper statements anymore. First of all, it's really bad for the planet. Think of the trees! Second, you probably need to look back at a paper statement once a year. You're really going to keep an entire filing cabinet filled with papers—papers you had to organize into individual folders—for the sixty seconds out of the year that you might need a single one of them? Really? No. **Shred old shit, opt in to paperless statements, and start fresh by keeping only the important shit you can't easily find online.**

Important papers that you can't always get on demand include medical directives and records, your most recent will and info for your executor, tax documents for the last seven years, deeds and birth certificates, and a list of the many, many accounts that characterize the slog of adulthood. That sounds like a lot, but it should be able to fit easily into a small fireproof safe. And it absolutely should be kept in a small fireproof safe. Whether you're dying, you have to leave your home in an emergency, or you just need the fifty-six kinds of identification the DMV now requires to get a fucking driver's license, you'll be glad to have everything in one secure place.

A pile of papers without labels helps no one

If you throw all of your papers, unsorted, into a filing cabinet or box like you're Nick Miller on *New Girl*, you've got bigger problems than paper statements. That is next-level chaos. Get your shit together.

There are certain things in life that only matter to you. If putting your cutlery in with your water glasses makes sense to you, more power to you. Although your guests will wonder whether you were drunk the last time you emptied your dishwasher, only you (and the people who live with you) need to know where to find things.

That's not how it works with important papers. If you're dead or incapacitated, someone will need quick and easy access to all the crap we've just covered. Presumably, you care about this person. Do you really want them tearing their hair out because they can't find your advance directive? If you live to face them, they may not let you live much longer. (It's worth noting that that cardboard box broke Nick and Jess up.) Buy a twelve-pack of colorful folders and a marker on Amazon, and get to fucking work.

ACCOUNTS
Your money goes more places than you do

Mortgage, water, sewer, gas, electric, insurance, car, cable, streaming services, memberships, credit cards— ain't adulting great? You pay a lot of bills. And when you're gone or indisposed or stuck in another country without your wallet, someone else is going to have to pay them or shut down the services they cover. Account names, numbers, and login credentials are a must. (Actually letting someone else log into those accounts is a bit of a gray area. But more on that in the next section.)

Make sure your executor or someone else who cares about you (and isn't likely to steal your identity) knows where they can find this info. In an emergency, you don't want to be trying to explain how to find shit over the phone. And that's if you're conscious and lucid. Add a morphine drip to this situation, and suddenly finding your insurance information is like some kind of TV game show Wayne Brady would host.

In the event of your death, you don't want grieving loved ones wondering how they're going to pay for services or getting unexpected bills. An organized and updated list of accounts is the bare fucking minimum you can give them to lighten their load. The best thing you can do is bake them some brownies and have a conversation about that list (chocolate makes every-thing better). Put those communication skills you've been learning throughout this death-cleaning shit to good use.

If you can't remember your passwords, your family's screwed

Logging into someone else's account is technically a no-no with most companies if you bother to read all that crap that you agree to when you sign up. So let me just say right now, **nothing in this book comes close to legal advice**. Talk to a lawyer before you access anyone's accounts or make plans for your own. But also, let he who's not sharing any streaming passwords cast the first stone. Sometimes, having that login info is the quickest way to get from A to B.

Most sites require a death certificate and some paperwork to shut things down. Some social media sites like Facebook let you designate a person, or "legacy contact," to deal with your account from the comfort of their own. I learned this when my grandmother passed and I realized I'd have to jump through fiery hoops to close her Facebook account. Thankfully, I had stored her login info when I set up her account, so I didn't have to rely on the Post-It Note she took with her to Georgia. I easily appointed myself legacy contact and memorialized her account. From A to B in minutes—just saying.

So first, a little homework: find out about the postmortem policies on your accounts. **Wherever you can, designate a beneficiary or point person now.** On second thought, make sure you get their permission first. An out-of-the-blue email telling someone you're appointing beneficiaries in the event of your death could scare the hell out of them.

Next, channel your inner Tolkien fan and use the "one password to rule them all" trick to save passwords in a way that A) isn't a pain in your ass when you need them, and B) doesn't leave them exposed to the known universe.* Use a file on your computer, an app on your phone, or a website expressly made for the purpose of collecting all your passwords in one place. Just make sure that whatever you use is password protected, and then pick a password that even the handiest hacker won't be able to fuck with. A long phrase that uses capital letters, lowercase letters, numbers, and characters is your safest bet. **It doesn't matter if this password is completely insane because**

---

*I don't know the numbers on people's password books being stolen, but they're not zero. Honestly, though, I don't think many people care enough to steal a password book unless it's lying in plain sight next to the MacBook they're really there to steal. But maybe your kid has sticky-fingered friends. If you have a physical book, at least put the damn thing in a locked drawer.

it's the only one you have to remember—one password to rule them all.

Most internet browsers work the same way, automatically saving your passwords and letting you look them up by entering your browser account password. They'll also alert you if those passwords get swiped and show up in some shady corner of the web. So, when Chrome asks if you want it to remember your password, just say yes. It beats the hell out of an Excel sheet.

BURN BOXES
Friends don't let friends' loved ones see their browsing history

If there's anything you wouldn't want your mother-in-law to spot during an unplanned visit or your kids to find after your gone, destroy it, secure it, or label it accordingly. If it's digital, appoint someone you trust to delete it. If it's physical, you're going to want a burn box.

A burn box is a container that's meant to be incinerated (or at least thrown away). If it's holding secrets or anything that would get an NC-17 rating, there should obviously be a lid. Or a zipper. Preferably a lock. Scrawling a simple "throw away without opening" somewhere on the box should do the trick.

Whether it's a grieving relative or just a curious toddler who happens upon your burn box, eventually someone will. Do what you've got to do to keep the trauma to a minimum all around. And if you think it's not traumatizing for your toddler to parade around with your vibrator in his little hands the moment your Ned Flanders–like neighbor decides to drop off your mail, think again. (It's also hilarious, though.) Of course, if you're dead, you're not going to give a damn what anyone finds. So go ahead and roll the dice, if that's your thing.

When you're the one who discovers the box, respect the warning. Finding a parent's nipple clamps after they've died may be the moment of levity you need while grieving, but some things are better left unimagined. And I'd seriously suggest wiping any browsing histories without looking at them. (Just don't clear any saved logins until you've gotten all the info you need on the accounts you have to pay and close.)

If it's family secrets and not sex toys you're hiding (hey, maybe it's both), consider coming clean rather than letting the truth die with you. You can do your best to keep your secrets, but that stuff has a way of seeping through the cracks. There are entire genres of movies devoted to what happens when the truth comes out.

Hopefully your secrets are a little more Hallmark than Lifetime, but, either way, deathbed confessions are a dick move. If you're at the center of the excitement, the least you can do is be around to answer questions about it. But if you'd rather take it to the grave, the smart move is to shred that shit yourself. Can't part with it? Label it "burn *before* reading."* Just know that not many people will be able to resist the sweet siren call of someone else's drama.

---

*Better yet, label it "socks to mend." They'll throw it right in the trash.

Some things are only important to you

If you want to hang onto a few things that make you happy, but you also don't want someone to have to deal with them later, you can sort them into a different kind of burn box. No lock or alarming warning required on this one. This burn box is for old photos, letters (of the PG variety), clippings, and mementos that only mean something to you. If your loved ones want to look through it, they can. (And they probably will. People are nosy as hell.) If they don't want to, they can toss the contents without a second thought.

Now, when I say "box," I'm not talking about one of those 45-gallon storage totes. I'm talking about a shoebox, *maybe* one of those cardboard filing boxes from an office-supply store. That should be relatively easy to manage because the stuff that survived decluttering is proudly displayed in your home. Right? (You better be nodding your head. We talked about this. It's not doing you a damn bit of good tucked away in an attic.) Once you have your box, be sure to label it "toss."

While you're at it, make a list of other items in your home that you'd be happy to have donated when you're gone. You can label things directly (a Post-It Note or sticky dot on the back or bottom of an object works) or leave instructions in your final arrangements. **Just find a way to be clear with your loved ones about what should be tossed when you're gone.** They might decide to keep some of those things in the end, or they might not. But at least they won't be wracked with guilt over the decision.

FINAL ARRANGEMENTS
Decision time—who gets the autographed baseball?

You've got your final wishes figured out, your funeral arrangements made, your executor named, and a guardian lined up for your betta fish. Great. Now what about all the crap in your house?

This is the part of estate planning that most people don't even think about. They think about the house, sure, but all the crap they've spent a lifetime collecting just seems to slip their minds. Not you, though. You've got all your ducks in a row and ready to file out at a moment's notice. Now is the time you decide on their marching orders.

Who gets what when you're gone? If you don't know, how the hell do you expect anyone else to? You're probably thinking, *I'm dead. What do I care*? Fair point. But we're cleaning up our own messes, right? And we're making sure our final act in this world isn't causing a family feud.

This is the last step, the home stretch, the lightning round. When you were decluttering, you started to think about who *might* get what and imagined what consequences each decision might cause. You did some digging and figured out where everyone stands. **You've pared down to the stuff you love and given away what you can. It's time to designate a survivor.** Ready? Who gets the fucking baseball?

See how stupid it sounds when I put it that way? You've done the hard part. Now stop overthinking it and start making a list.

Your loved ones can't read your fucking mind

I don't care if you've got a waffle maker, a bitchy houseplant, and twenty dollars to your name. If you want any say in where that waffle maker ends up, you have to put it in writing. You can't just think it once and hope it works out.

For smaller things, you can put together an informal letter to tuck in with your will. This is where you'll include your account information, donation instructions, tips for how to care for that persnickety fiddle-leaf fig, a list of who's getting your most-prized-yet-worthless possessions, and any deathbed confessions you'd like to get off your chest. (Kidding on that last one. Mostly.)

Just keep in mind that this isn't a legal document, and your executor isn't obligated to abide by it. That's a lesson in both legality and assholery. Choose your executor wisely. (And make sure they're not a featured player in that deathbed confession.)

The valuable stuff, like your car or your wedding ring, gets added to your will. You'll need to name specific beneficiaries and backup beneficiaries for each item. You could also opt for a blanket "I leave all my worldly possessions to my neighbor, Joann." But your will won't be settled until after your funeral, and someone needs to water that damn plant in the meantime.

If you've got serious assets—money, property, racehorses—you may want to look into trusts. They can help ensure your shit goes where you want it to, and possibly without the lengthy court processes. But if you've got waffle-maker money, a will should be fine.

Hopefully you've got many happy, healthy years ahead of you to enjoy your stuff. **This is about creating a foundation that makes that long life easier.** Then, a few times a year, you can spend five minutes making sure everything's updated and get on with it.

Give your kids permission to throw it all out

Even when you've done your due diligence, decluttered completely, and carefully selected which kid gets what based on their own feedback, your stuff could still end up on the curb. Maybe someone changed their mind, or maybe they were only telling you what you wanted to hear. Maybe they realized they physically couldn't get that couch up the fucking stairs in their fifth-floor walkup, even with all the pivoting that Ross Geller could muster.

If you've followed the advice in this book and done the work, you can rest easy knowing you've done the best you could. Whatever happens next is not your problem or responsibility. Plus, you'll be beyond caring at that point.*

---

*If you believe in an afterlife and really think you'll be sitting there (whichever direction *there* is), giving a shit about what happens to your *Alice in Wonderland* chess set, you need more help than this book can give you. Or maybe you just need a more interesting afterlife.

With that in mind, let your kids off the hook. Let them know you're truly OK with them getting rid of everything you've left behind. You're not going to haunt Miguel if he sells your comic-book collection for cash or fault Emma for not letting your LEGOs go from your basement to hers. **Once you're gone, that stuff is theirs to do with as they please.**

Make it clear that your love and approval is not contingent upon them keeping your shit. This simple, generous act can break the clutter cycle, free your kids from guilt and shame, and give them a chance to enjoy all those benefits we talked about in Chapter 1. And it'll keep them from spitting on your grave. (Hey, if that's what matters most to you, I'm not judging. Whatever gets you to clean out your garage.)

CLUE IN ANYONE WHO NEEDS TO KNOW WHERE YOU KEEP THE GOODS

All that important paperwork we've talked about—the bills, the streaming logins, the will, the plant-care instructions? It's not worth a damn if no one knows where to find it. This isn't a "put it away for safe-keeping" kind of situation. Whenever you do that with a birthday present or key card, those fuckers are never seen again.

This is a "filed with the lawyer and copied in the fireproof safe" situation. But, again, you're going to need to let someone into your little circle of trust—namely, the executor and the alternate executor. (Yes, like a hockey player subbing in for the guy who took a puck to the teeth. Odds are good your bestie was standing right next to you when that bus jumped the curb.)

Let's say your partner is your executor, and your daughter (the one who can load a dishwasher*) is your alternate. If those are the only two people you trust, I don't blame you. People are shady as fuck. But if you're lucky enough to have a wider circle, let them in. You never know who's going to be handy in an emergency.

Whether your documents are protected by a password, a key, or a combination, make sure everyone who needs it has it or knows where they can find it. Personally, I like a good mystery key—the kind you keep because you know it's important, but you have no earthly idea what it unlocks. Someday, your best friend will need to get into your safe (to get bail money for you after you clocked that haggler at your yard sale) and realize she had the key all along.

---

*I just want to give a shout-out to anyone who gets my little callbacks to earlier sections. I see you, and I appreciate you.

PASS DOWN THE STORIES, NOT THE STUFF

Some things are simply useful, like a laundry basket or a lamp. We keep them around because we need them. But most things in life we keep because they stir up memories and emotions, which is precisely why we're so loath to get rid of a single fucking pen. They help us experience the full spectrum of emotions and process our journeys on this spinning rock.

One of the most important gifts we can give ourselves and our loved ones is to separate the memory from the thing. We're hardwired to conflate the two. But you can share your memories long after a thing is gone. A lot of the time, the memories are better. How big was that fish you caught last summer? Exactly.

Without the memory, a thing is just a thing. Your kids find an old, beat-up sled at the back of the garage and think nothing of adding it to the trash heap because you didn't tell them what it meant to you. They don't know the story of your father, the stoic war veteran, gleefully gliding down hills with you in his lap and plowing, sled-first, into a tree at the bottom. If you tell them, you could get rid of the sled, and they'd still have the story.

As you declutter, revel in those memories. Soak them up. Let yourself feel the emotions they evoke. **Call up your loved ones and tell them the stories that come to mind, or jot them down to enjoy later. Then let that shit go. The story's what matters.**

REALIZE THAT YOUR INBOX WILL NEVER BE EMPTY

Even if you lived to be 102, you couldn't check every little thing off your to-do list. But at that point, you're probably pretty well out of fucks about it. In the mean-time, just do the best you can with what you've got.

If you've got a house full of stuff, chip away at it. Every little bit helps. If you've got big plans for that stuff, get on it. Reaching 102 is a pipe dream—you barely drink enough water to reach the end of the day. The point is, as always, that you have to find what works for you.

You're never going to be done decluttering (mostly because you keep hitting up TJ Maxx). You can let your eternal to-do list bum you out, or you can embrace the lack of clear deadline like the true procrastinator I know you are. If the job is never done, then you don't need to feel guilty about taking breaks. And you don't need to worry about making everything perfect.

You can also stop to smell the roses along the way, which will help keep burnout at bay. Get the family together for that stroll down Memory Lane before you purge your photo collection. Tell your kids all about your gnarliest childhood injuries. Bust out those old Rollerblades and hit the pavement. (Not literally. You're older now. You can't bounce back from a broken arm the way you used to.)

We don't have endless amounts of time on this planet, and it'll just keep rotating without us. The only thing we can do is find a way to balance planning and acting with resting and enjoying. The clutter will be there tomorrow. And the next day. And the one after that . . .

Chapter 4 Checklist

☐ Clean up your fucking mess so your kids don't have to

☐ Don't put the burden of making decisions on your kids

☐ Put some careful thought into divvying up your shit

☐ Get used to the idea that your kids have their own taste

☐ Gift the important shit while you're still alive to do it

☐ Spend five minutes decluttering your desktop

☐ Make a habit of clearing your browsing history

☐ Switch to paperless statements like you live in the twenty-first century

☐ Ditch the file cabinet in favor of one small fireproof safe

☐ Organize your fucking papers

- [ ] Have all your account info in one secure place
- [ ] Use one password to protect all the others and free up some fucking brain cells
- [ ] Label shit your family can toss guilt-free
- [ ] Label shit your family should toss without looking at
- [ ] Make a damn decision and put it in writing
- [ ] Tell a few trusted people where to find the important shit
- [ ] Tell the stories that are important to you
- [ ] Take time to enjoy the process and avoid burnout
- [ ] Do the best you can, then let that shit go

5

Live Your Damn Life
(Clutter Free)

TAKE IN ALL THAT UNCLUTTERED GLORY

You've made it! You've powered through your own bullshit, made a plan, followed through, built up those "fuck it" muscles, and gotten your ducks in a row. Or at least you've read about doing all those things. Hey, progress is progress.*

Hopefully these pages have inspired you to dig into this whole death-cleaning thing, and you're starting to see some results. There's nothing like the warm glow of triumph coming off a clutter-free makeup cabinet or perfectly curated closet. Just imagine how it's going to feel when you finally finish clearing out the basement and start in on that home theater. Or gym. Whatever.

With every section you declutter, you take back a little more control over your life. (You lost it to your kids, job, and societal pressure somewhere in the early

---

*A lot of people never pick up another book after high school. You're reading one that calls you on your shit. That alone is admirable.

nineties. It misses you.) This is your life, your home, your happiness. You're in charge. And, from now on, you're going to be more mindful about what you allow to come into your home.

The good news is, you've already done the hard work. You've laid the foundation. At this point, fucking it up is going to be harder than maintaining it. But if you need a little help, this chapter's got you covered.

REVEL IN THOSE BENEFITS YOU'VE BEEN WORKING TOWARD

Take a few minutes to look around at the spaces you've uncluttered and the progress you've made. (Go ahead. I'll wait right here.) Check you out! You are a self-aware, decision-making badass. Take it in.

How does your space feel now compared to how it felt when you started? Really sit with it for a minute. How do *you* feel? Noticing any of those benefits we talked about in Chapter 1? Better sleep, more energy and creativity, less anxiety, fewer things to clean, a deeper appreciation for your space? You should be ticking at least a few of these boxes by now.

If you think you're reaping those benefits at home, just wait until you start noticing them out in the world. More self-confidence, better decision-making skills, clearer priorities—that is the stuff of life-changing magic. Take that shit to work with you, or to the grocery store the next time someone reaches for the last perfectly ripe avocado. You can do anything you put your mind to.

Best of all, you get to come home to a space you love, one that fits you perfectly and lights you up. That joyful energy is contagious. That's the legacy you get to pass down to your loved ones. And it's a hell of a lot better than a collection of creepy-ass garden gnomes.

USE SOME FUCKING COMMON SENSE

Your memory might not get much worse, but it sure as hell isn't going to get any better. Do you want to spend the rest of your life scrambling to find your keys like you do now? Develop a good system today, and it'll last you the rest of your life.

You don't have to reinvent the wheel here. You already instinctively put a lot of stuff where you need it, like your phone charger by the bed and your dog's leash by the door. You just need to do it on purpose. Carve out a little space for your phone and glasses on the nightstand and hang a hook for the dog's leash. See? Not rocket science.

Now think about the things you lose over and over again, like your earbuds. Time to solve the fucking problem once and for all. If you have to keep your earbud case charging in the laundry room to remind you to take the fucking things out of your pocket before you wash them again, then that's what you do. Get creative. Try Velcro. Just figure out what works for you.

Once you have a place for everything, the last piece of the puzzle is remembering to consistently put things back where they belong. Things tend to wander—sunglasses, keys, scissors. If you spend literally three minutes a day putting shit away, you'll add years to your life that would have been wasted on irrational anger about stubbed toes and missing remotes. And maybe your earbuds will survive more than a week.

MAKE BETTER CHOICES
Remember why you did all this in the first place

You've heard of lifestyle creep? The more money you earn, the more you spend. It works the same way with your stuff. The more space you have, the more you fill. We're done with that shit. A little open space is a good thing. It's good for your mental health, and it keeps you from running into the corners of coffee tables (and then wondering a week later how you got that crazy bruise).

Whenever you start to resist or fall back into old habits, come back to your why. Look at how far it's gotten you. And remember, you're not just doing this for you. You're doing it for the people who love you and desperately don't want to clean out a garage full of roadside freebies when you're gone. You get a clean garage and your sanity; they get to remember you fondly. Win-win.

Put some mental effort in before you buy sh*t

One of the easiest ways to keep your home clutter free? Stop buying shit. Of course, that's easier said than done, especially if you're used to buying what you need on a whim.

First, you have to redefine "need." Do you really need that fancy digital, glow-in-the-dark tire-pressure gauge, or will the old pencil version do the job? Do you need another fucking candle when you already have twelve tucked away in various cabinets, waiting for the right season?

When you have money to spare, the definition of "need" tends to expand. But clearing the clutter isn't about saving money (although that is a super handy side effect). It's about knowing the value of your space. And you know those needs need to be earning their keep.

When you're tempted to hit "buy now," interrupt the cycle. Imagine putting that money toward an experience you've been dreaming about. You'll be shocked by how quickly your impulse purchases add up to real money you can use for stuff that's way more fulfilling than a pressure gauge or another pumpkin-scented candle.

LOOK FOR DECLUTTERING OPPORTUNITIES—THEY'RE EVERYWHERE!

Know someone who's just starting out and could use that rice cooker that's been taking up precious kitchen-cabinet space?* Can you volunteer to work your neighbor's yard sale for a few hours in exchange for some table space? Stumble across a family heirloom you know your daughter would love? Seize moments like these to ditch even more clutter.

Decluttering never stops, even after you're dead. But once you've done the heavy lifting, you can relax into the process. **Just let the decluttering current take you wherever it's going.** Every time you come across an object in your home, you have the opportunity to

---

*Remember: we're not foisting stuff on loved ones without asking anymore. Round up a bunch of stuff you'd be willing to part with and let them pick what they want. You could even take this "living in the moment" stuff to heart and make a lovely afternoon of it. Let the free stuff be the icing on the cake. After enjoying actual cake.

ask yourself: Do you need it? Do you use it? Does it make you happy? Will it make someone else happier?

Here's a little secret: You don't need to be in decluttering mode to declutter something. One day, you grab some earrings out of your jewelry box and notice a necklace you're not wild about anymore. You can offer it to a friend, sell it online, or take it to a thrift store that same day, all by itself. The instinct to declutter is inside you. Just let it do its thing.

LIGHT A FIRE UNDER THE ASSES OF RELUCTANT FAMILY MEMBERS

When it comes to broaching the subject of death cleaning with parents or older relatives, timing is everything. No grown-ass person wants to be talked to like they're a child in need of guardrails. But you need to talk about safety way before you really *need* to talk about safety. Telling someone their shag carpeting is a tripping hazard when they're still mobile enough to find it funny is going to be far more effective than saying it when they're pissed off about their lack of mobility.

If you're going to gain any traction at all, you need to start talking about it now. Just have a conversation. In fact, have a lot of them. **You don't need to browbeat your parents into throwing out all of their beloved belongings. Just ask them the same questions you've been asking yourself.** What makes you happy? What are you getting sick of dealing with? How much can you get for that antique rain lamp when they're gone? (Kidding. Mostly.*)

Older folks aren't the only ones who need this. No one knows when their time is up, so it's never too early to get your ducks in a row. And if you can keep them in line, your life will be happier and easier. (And your death will incur far less resentment from those left behind.) Keep in mind, also, that women live longer than men. Look around. Do you want to deal with

---

*Sometimes, showing a person they can make a little extra scratch from stuff they're not that attached to can help motivate them to deal with it. Be careful what you wish for, though—you're probably going to end up doing the heavy lifting for any online sales.

all your husband's shit when he's gone? Get his ass moving now. Declutter together, or save your marriage and declutter separately. But get to work.

GET ALL THE FAMILY TEA WHILE YOU CAN

Going through the death-cleaning process with a family member can be one of the most frustrating, pain-in-the-ass experiences of your life. But it can also be more cathartic than therapy. Maybe you bond over finding a long-lost recipe for your grandmother's cinnamon buns in her own handwriting or learning all about your dad's time overseas. Maybe you even break through some generational trauma. It's like emotional *Wheel of Fortune*—you never know where you're going to land!

This is a great time to ask any questions you might have and to listen to whatever stories there are to tell. You might pull out a photo of the aunt you never got to know and learn that you get your love of animals from her. Or that it's entirely possible she was the love child of your grandmother and her first fiancé. You never know what drama you'll dig up when decluttering long-forgotten boxes that have been passed from generation to generation.

The thing is, you don't know what you don't know. One day, a question will pop into your head, and there'll be no one left to answer it. Take the opportunity death cleaning presents to learn as much as you can now, while there's still time to enjoy the shared schadenfreude of Uncle Jimmy's hilariously awful magician phase.

FILL THE REST OF YOUR LIFE WITH EXPERIENCES, NOT STUFF

You know where you won't need that twelve-piece dining set you got for your wedding and never took out of the hutch? On a beach in Fiji. Or a gondola in

Venice. Or a hike in Yellowstone. Want to move to Portland and live out your food-truck fantasy? Just imagine how easy packing is going to be now that you've done all the heavy lifting. Fewer things mean more freedom—financial and physical—to do whatever the hell you want with the rest of your life.

Even if you don't travel the world with your retirement, you can choose to spend your money on *doing* instead of *having*. Head to the park for the day, host a family dinner, go to the movies. With all the money you'll be saving on stuff you don't need, you'll no longer need to take out a second mortgage to afford a small popcorn and soda. Just don't bring home any souvenirs from your days out on the town. What have we learned? That's right: things are not memories.

CUT YOURSELF SOME SLACK ONCE IN A WHILE

Yes, you will have to keep decluttering for the rest of your life. You're human. You're going to buy shit you don't need. But your whole life doesn't have to be about death cleaning.

Remember, we're aiming for happy, not perfect. **Changing a few of your *ahem* less-than-helpful habits can go a long way toward a happy life.** But so can buying the occasional piece of seasonal décor. Life is short, and this one's yours.

LIVE (PROBABLY LONGER) WITHOUT REGRET OR GUILT

Imagine that you've worked through this book and finally checked "organize the fucking house" off your to-do list. What are you going to do with all your free time now that you have your shit together? ("Go shopping" isn't an option, smart-ass.) You haven't just cleared out some clutter and made a little cash on vintage LPs. You've worked through some pretty heavy mental and emotional shit too.

You may have started this process out of guilt about the mess you might have left behind. But you've stepped up. You're taking responsibility for your decisions, rebuilding your relationships, and generally taking life by the balls. That's all you. You get to take those skills with you and use them in everything you do from here on out.

You know by now that your work is never finished, but you've done the hard part. It gets so much fucking easier from here. Just keep going. Keep calling yourself on your bullshit, separating the stuff from the memories, and coming back to what lights you up. And in the process, you'll build the life you've always wanted. **It's never too late to start fresh.**

Chapter 5 Checklist

☐ Notice how good it feels to have your shit together

☐ Enjoy taking those badass decision-making skills for a spin in the real world

☐ Spend five fucking minutes a day putting things where they belong

☐ Remember why you're doing this in the first place

☐ Check those buying habits before you wreck your clutter-free space

☐ Let your decluttering instincts take over (you have those now!)

☐ Walk your loved ones through the same process you've worked through

☐ Use death cleaning as an opportunity to learn more about your loved ones

☐ Catch flights, not freebies

☐ Make small changes to your habits to help big changes stick

☐ Pat yourself on the back for getting your shit together